W9-CZW-648

MAR

2011

FACTS AT YOUR FINGERTIPS

REPRODUCTION AND GENETICS

BROWN
BEAR
BOOKS

Published by Brown Bear Books Limited

4877 N. Circulo Bujia
Tucson, AZ 85718
USA

and

First Floor
9-17 St. Albans Place
London N1 ONX
UK
www.brownreference.com

Library of Congress Cataloging-in-Publication Data

Reproduction and genetics / edited by Sarah Eason.
    p. cm. – (Facts at your fingertips)
  Includes index.
  ISBN 978-1-936333-00-4 (lib. bdg.)
 1. Human reproduction–Juvenile literature. 2. Human
genetics–Juvenile literature. I. Eason, Sarah. II. Title. III.
Series.

  QP251.5.R47 2010
  612.6–dc22

                                            2010015186

ISBN-13 978-1-936333-00-4

Editorial Director: Lindsey Lowe
Editor: Sarah Eason
Proofreader: Jolyon Goddard
Designer: Paul Myerscough
Design Manager: David Poole
Children's Publisher: Anne O'Daly
Production Director: Alastair Gourlay

Printed in the United States of America

Picture Credits

Abbreviations: b=bottom; c=center; t=top; l=left; r=right.

Front Cover: Shutterstock: Spectral Design
Back Cover: Shutterstock: Kentoh

Istockphoto: Armin Hinterwirth 45, Henrik Jonsson 6;
Shutterstock: Benis Arapovic 32, BG_Knight 23, Rich Carey
43, Cre8tive Images 4, Cuson 9, Andrea Danti 26, Victoria
Field 25, Forster Forest 60, Four Oaks 13, Tyler Fox 47,
Christopher Futcher 59, Mandy Godbehear 36, Victor
Habbick 5, Chris K Horne 8, iofoto 14, Sebastian Kaulitzki
29, 31, Knorre 20, Nadezhda V. Kulagina 57, Mopic 48,
Steve McWilliam 10, Glenda M. Powers 61, Paul Prescott
54, Dr. Morley Read 35, Hugo Rocha 34, Ronfromyork 16,
Stana 1, 40, Michael Taylor 56, Vladimir Wrangel 39,
Dmitry Yatsenko 3.

Artwork © The Brown Reference Group Ltd

*The Brown Reference Group Ltd has made every effort to
trace copyright holders of the pictures used in this book.
Anyone having claims to ownership not identified above is
invited to contact The Brown Reference Group Ltd.*

CONTENTS

WHAT IS REPRODUCTION?

All living things reproduce by having young, or offspring. All individuals will die sooner or later, from disease, accident, predation, or environmental change. So, species can only survive if members reproduce (have young).

The ways animals produce young are as diverse as Earth's life-forms themselves: Some creatures lay eggs, and others give birth to live young; some species have males and females, while other species do not; some animals can change from male to female or vice versa, while other life-forms, such as bacteria, simply divide in two. Despite these differences, reproduction can be divided into two types: sexual and asexual.

Sexual reproduction involves the fusion of a male and female **sex cell** (a **sperm** and an **egg**).

Fertilization occurs when one male sperm cell penetrates the outer membrane of the female egg. The fertilized egg, now known as a zygote, rapidly divides to make more cells.

This is **fertilization**. A fertilized egg grows into a new individual. Since each sex cell carries half of the mom's or dad's **genes**, new individuals have their own unique combinations of genes. This creates genetic (inherited) variety. Humans reproduce sexually. **Asexual reproduction** creates offspring that are genetically identical to their parent—they all have exactly the same genes.

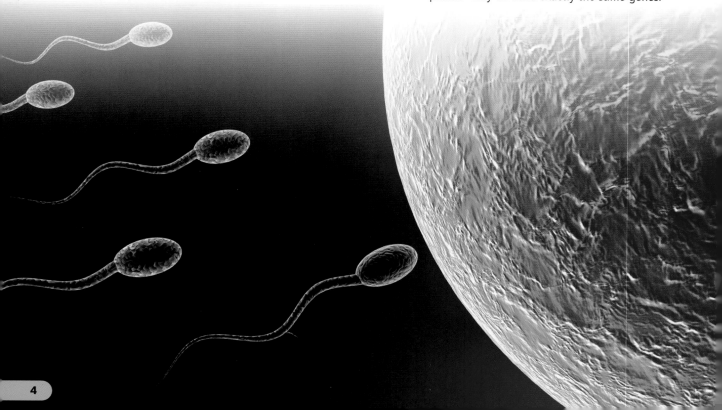

Studying reproduction

The scientific study of **reproduction** draws together many areas of biology. Genetics (the study of **inheritance**) and cell biology explain what occurs at the microscopic level. Reproductive physiology investigates how the body's reproductive systems work. Theories of reproduction are important in evolutionary biology, which traces how life-forms arose and evolved (changed over long periods time). An understanding of reproduction is also important for agriculture and medicine.

The study of reproduction and growth raises many questions. Some of them we now have answers to, but others are still a mystery. For example, the processes of fertilization and of how sex **hormones** work are now basically understood, but other details are still to be figured out. For instance, although new facts about aging have been uncovered, a great deal remains unknown.

There are also many intriguing "Why?" questions. Why, for example, are there separate male and female individuals? Why reproduce sexually at all? Why do some living things reproduce only once and others many times? Practical issues raised by the study of inheritance are equally wide-ranging: What can we do about human infertility? Why do things sometimes go wrong during development? Can we slow down or reverse the aging process? And if so, how?

SCIENCE WORDS

- **asexual reproduction** Any type of reproduction that produces offspring without involving mating or fertilization.
- **fertilization** The fusion of a sperm and an egg. It can occur externally (inside a body), as in mammals, or externally (outside the body), as in many fish.
- **gene** A segment of deoxyribonucleic acid (DNA). Chromosomes, which are made of DNA and so carry genes, are passed from parents to offspring by the sex cells. Genes control the development and growth of physical features.

FARMING TO SCIENCE

In the 18th century animal and plant breeders probably had a more accurate idea of reproduction and inheritance than scientists did. This was the time of the Agricultural Revolution, when improved breeds of cattle, sheep, and crop plants were being created. The breeders often kept their methods secret to protect their profits. Their experience inspired both Charles Darwin's (1809–1882) evolutionary theories and Gregor Mendel's (1822–1884) studies of genetics.

ASEXUAL REPRODUCTION

In simple terms, asexual reproduction is any reproduction that does not involve the fusion of sex cells. In more detail, asexual reproduction produces new individuals that are genetically identical to the parent.

Ordinary cell division, or **mitosis**, is a type of asexual reproduction. But the term asexual reproduction is most commonly used when discussing whole organisms and how they reproduce (have young). The majority of single-celled life-forms reproduce asexually, including bacteria and many protists. The first life on Earth was single celled. For millions of years until sexual reproduction evolved, asexual

Most bacteria reproduce by a process known as binary fission. One cell splits and forms two identical daughter cells. Binary fission gives a population of bacteria the potential to double every 20 minutes.

reproduction was the only way for life-forms to make copies of themselves.

Today many species never reproduce sexually, not just single-celled life-forms. Many plants and a number of animals reproduce asexually. Some reproduce sexually and asexually, and have complex **life cycles**. Asexual reproduction takes many forms, from the simple splitting of a cell or body (**fission**) to the use of specialized reproductive structures such as **spores**.

What's the difference?

The key difference between sexual and asexual reproduction is that one produces individuals with unique combinations of genes, and the other does not.

Genes are segments of **deoxyribonucleic acid (DNA)**. They carry the instructions for life: Genes dictate how a cell divides to multiply and what **proteins** are made. Proteins are the building blocks

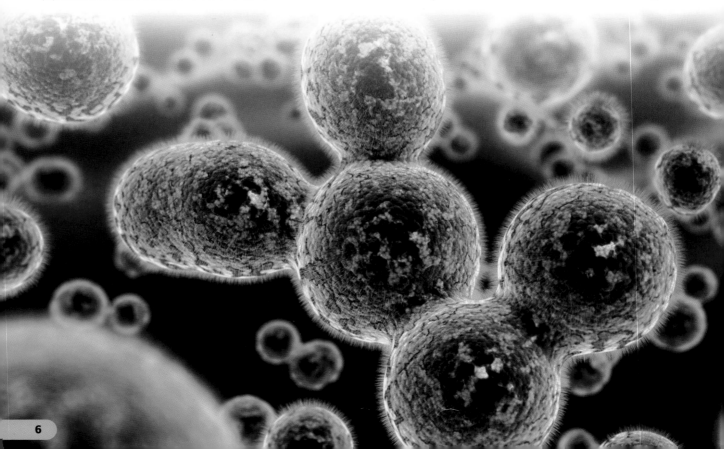

SPORES

Spores are tiny, specialized reproductive structures produced by many nonflowering plants. Spores are much smaller than most seeds and contain only one or a few cells surrounded by a protective coating. Spores are small enough to blow in the wind. In the right conditions they germinate (sprout) into new plants. Unlike seeds, spores are usually produced asexually, though often this is part of a complex life cycle that also includes a sexual stage. Mushrooms and other fungi produce both sexual and asexual spores.

The **pollen** grains of flowering plants probably evolved from spores. Pollen only "germinates" when it reaches the female part of a flower—then the male sex cells within the pollen grow toward the flower's egg-containing ovaries.

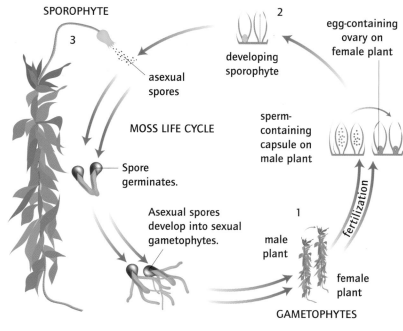

SPOROPHYTE

asexual spores

MOSS LIFE CYCLE

Spore germinates.

Asexual spores develop into sexual gametophytes.

developing sporophyte

egg-containing ovary on female plant

sperm-containing capsule on male plant

fertilization

male plant

female plant

GAMETOPHYTES

A sperm from a male moss fertilizes (fuses with) an egg on a female moss (1). These sexual stages are gametophytes. The asexual sporophyte develops (2) from the fertilized female. It releases asexual spores (3) that become gametophytes (1).

of life. They control what an organism looks like and how it works. DNA coils to form **chromosomes**. Every type of life-form has a set number of chromosomes. People have 46.

For new offspring to exist successfully, they need to receive a complete set of chromosomes from their parents. Sexually reproducing organisms receive a random half of their chromosomes from their mother, and another half from their father. That ensures each new individual will have a unique combination of chromosomes and hence unique genes. Asexually reproducing organisms get all their DNA from just one parent. So, these organisms are genetically identical to that parent. Genetically identical offspring are called **clones**.

Fission

Simple asexual reproduction by the division of a cell into two separate and similar parts is called binary fission. Bacteria divide in this way to reproduce. Binary fission involves a doubling of the cell's genetic (inherited) material, or DNA. Each new cell takes half of the doubled DNA. This leaves both new cells with the same amount of DNA as the parent cell.

Some algae and protozoans regularly divide by multiple fission: The DNA-containing **nucleus** of a cell divides by mitosis several times. This creates a number of nuclei, each with the same amount of DNA as the original nucleus. After the nucleus has finished dividing, the rest of the cell separates around each nucleus to form individual cells. Some algal cells produce spores by multiple fission.

Asexuality in plants

In plants there is often no clear division between asexual (or vegetative) reproduction and normal growth processes. For example, many plants, such as

TRY THIS

Testing Out Plants

Are most plants able to grow asexually from cuttings? And if so, can they grow from leaves or only from stems or roots? Try planting out small pieces of wild plants or (with permission) houseplants. Keep them watered for a few weeks. How many have taken root? Where nothing has happened, does this prove that they cannot grow from cuttings at all, or could there be other explanations? Does the ability to grow from cuttings relate to what you know of the plant's lifestyle in the wild?

the marshland reeds, spread by buried stems that grow out sideways. New shoots and roots sprout from these buried stems. So a single "plant" can sometimes cover many acres. But each part can act as a separate plant if the connection with the "mother" is broken. Other plants, such as strawberries, produce sideways-growing overground stems called runners. Where their ends touch the ground, the runners root and grow into new plants. Some plants can also spread from small fragments.

Plants also have specialized structures for asexual reproduction, including tiny spores. Spores are transported by the wind. Many simple plants such as mosses, as well as reproducing sexually, grow small bundles of cells called gemmae. Gemmae are produced asexually. They are spread by raindrops and grow into new plants.

Asexual animals

Many invertebrates (animals without a backbone) reproduce asexually. Often buds form that break away from the parent to then become separate individuals. Asexual reproduction is common in soft-bodied sea animals such as bryozoans, sponges, cnidarians (corals, sea anemones, and relatives), echinoderms (starfish and relatives), and also many aquatic worms. Animals like corals attach to a single spot and filter food from the water. Often individuals do not separate completely from their parent, and

WHAT IS AN INDIVIDUAL?

Some colonial animals, which live in groups, reproduce asexually but do not completely separate from each other, such as corals. Would you describe them as made of separate joined individuals or as a single individual with many mouths? Why? In some animal colonies there is division of labor between different units in the colony. Some members are responsible for feeding, others for reproduction, and others for defense. Would that make a difference in your answer?

Starfish can reproduce asexually in a process called fragmentation. If part of an arm becomes detached, it can develop into a new individual. The parent then regenerates a new arm.

large connected colonies form. Reef-building corals make such colonies. It is no coincidence that such animals are often good at regenerating (replacing lost or damaged parts); similar processes are involved in regeneration and asexual reproduction.

Virgin births

The word *parthenogenesis* comes from the Greek word for "virgin birth." The word refers to a kind of asexual reproduction in which young develop from unfertilized eggs. Eggs are not normally involved in asexual reproduction. They are vital to sexual reproduction, though, in which a sperm fertilizes (fuses with) an egg. The eggs of sexually reproducing creatures carry half of the mother's chromosomes. However, the eggs of organisms that reproduce by parthenogenesis carry a full set of chromosomes. So there is no need for sperm to provide the missing half. Organisms that reproduce in this way probably descended from sexual organisms. At some point in their evolution something, such as a lack of males, made switching to asexual reproduction beneficial.

Some lizard species have all-female populations and reproduce by parthenogenesis, which produces clones of the parent. Komodo dragons can reproduce parthenogenetically if there are no males to breed with.

SCIENCE WORDS

- **deoxyribonucleic acid (DNA)** Molecule that contains the genetic code for all cellular (nonvirus) organisms.
- **fission** A type of asexual reproduction used by single-celled life-forms. In binary fission one cell divides into two. In multiple fission one cell divides into more than two daughter cells.
- **parthenogenesis** A type of asexual reproduction in which live young develop from unfertilized eggs. Means "virgin birth."
- **spore** An asexual reproductive cell that can develop into a new individual without being fertilized. Spores are produced by bacteria, fungi, and green plants.

SEXUAL REPRODUCTION

Sexual reproduction creates individuals that inherit a mixture of genes from more than one parent. The incredible variety of sexual behaviors, structures, and interrelations in the natural world all help achieve this.

A male and female make contact with each other and **mate**. Later on, the female gives birth to live young or lays fertilized eggs. This is most people's image of sexual reproduction, but it is only one of many different patterns in nature. In many species male and female never meet; indeed, there are often no separate males and females at all. For organisms made of many cells, such as animals and plants, sexual reproduction also means that at some stage in their life cycle they have to return to being a single cell.

Adult frogs adopt a position called amplexus when they mate. The male (on top) grasps the female around her chest with his forelegs. The pair then releases eggs and sperm into the water, where external fertilization occurs.

WHY HAVE SEX?

Why sex exists at all is one of the hottest topics in biology. Around 99 percent of all animal species reproduce sexually, so sex must have big advantages for animals. Sex creates variety in offspring by mixing the genes of different parents. In the long term variety is good since it helps a species adapt to challenges in the future. The problem is how to square this with the way scientists believe natural selection works. According to selfish gene theory, an individual is only concerned with the survival of its own genes, not with the good of the species as a whole. A female animal that reproduces by parthenogenesis ought therefore to be at an advantage, because all her genes are passed on to each offspring, not just half of them. Some scientists think that for sex to exist, it must have short-term advantages as well—perhaps because genetic variety helps life-forms keep one step ahead of parasites such as bacteria and viruses.

TRY THIS

Male or Female?
Have a good look at the birds and other animals around your neighborhood. Can you tell apart the males and females of different species? What differences can you spot in their size, appearance, and behavior? Using reference books at a library or the Internet, check to see whether you guessed right. If you were wrong, was it because you were thinking of them in human terms? When males and females do differ, can you relate this to the way the creatures reproduce?

Fertilization

In animals, male sex cells are called spermatozoa or sperm, and female sex cells are called egg cells or ova (singular ovum). Egg cells vary hugely in size depending on how much yolk they contain but are always much bigger than sperm cells. Sperm also vary but in most species they are tadpole-shaped. The head contains the sperm's tightly packed chromosomes and is attached to a long tail (flagellum) for propulsion.

When a sperm reaches an egg, the sperm releases **enzymes** that help it penetrate the egg's outer layers. Fertilization occurs when the head of

the sperm is taken into the egg. Development can then begin. Once fertilized, the egg puts up chemical barriers that prevent any more sperm from entering.

*When a sperm fertilizes (fuses with) an egg (1), cell division is triggered. As the fertilized egg, or zygote (2), divides, it increases in size and complexity, eventually forming an **embryo**. The egg's outer coat of cells disappears soon after fertilization. In mammals, the inner layer of gel remains until the zygote enters the uterus, around six days after fertilization. Both these layers protect the egg.*

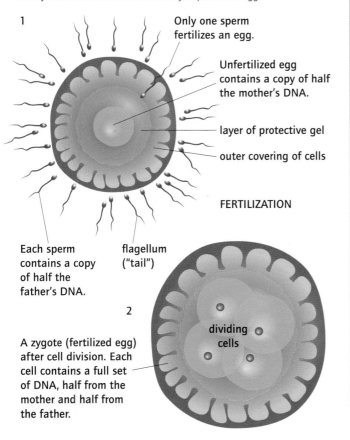

1

Only one sperm fertilizes an egg.

Unfertilized egg contains a copy of half the mother's DNA.

layer of protective gel

outer covering of cells

FERTILIZATION

Each sperm contains a copy of half the father's DNA.

flagellum ("tail")

2

dividing cells

A zygote (fertilized egg) after cell division. Each cell contains a full set of DNA, half from the mother and half from the father.

Animal reproductive systems

Most animals produce sperm and eggs inside sex organs called gonads. A gonad that produces sperm is called a testis (plural, testes), while an egg-producing gonad is called an ovary. There is also usually a duct or tube that carries the sperm or eggs to the outside, as well as somewhere to store the sex cells before they are released. Some males also have adaptations, such as a penis, that place their sperm inside the female's body. Similarly, females often have structures for egg laying or for giving birth to live young.

Some parts of the reproductive system do not develop fully until sexual maturity. In people and other vertebrates hormones (chemical messengers) from the brain target the sex organs. In turn, the sex organs produce other hormones such as **testosterone** (in males) and **estrogen** (in females). These sex hormones trigger the development of sex-specific characteristics, such as breasts in women and beards in men, and also maintain the production of eggs or sperm.

In different types of vertebrates the same sex hormones tend to occur, but their effects vary from one animal type to another. Prolactin, for example, is a hormone that promotes milk production in female mammals. In birds, however, it has other effects, including triggering egg-incubating behavior.

Estrus and menstrual cycles

The monthly female cycle in which eggs are released (the menstrual cycle) occurs only in people and some other primates, including other apes and monkeys.

A related cycle called the estrus cycle takes place in other mammals. These cycles are maintained by complex systems of hormonal control, and some are also influenced by the seasons.

SEX IN PLANTS

Plants face many of the reproductive problems faced by animals, especially those that live on land. Ancient land plants such as mosses and ferns have male sex cells similar to animal sperm cells. Their sperm also have flagella, moving tails that allow them to swim through water. For this reason most of these nonflowering plants only live in wet places. Splashes of rainwater enable the male sex cells to swim from one plant to another.

Part of the success of flowering plants is that they do not rely on a wet environment for reproduction. They achieve fertilization using pollen grains. Pollen is tough and resistant to desiccation (drying out). When a pollen grain reaches the female part of a flower (1), the grain sprouts and grows a tube down to the **ovary** inside (2–3). The pollen then releases a male sex cell that travels to and fuses with a female sex cell in the ovary (4). The fertilized egg then begins to grow into an embryo, which eventually becomes a seed (5).

Because plants cannot move around to mate, they use animals such as insects, bats, or birds, or the wind to carry their pollen.

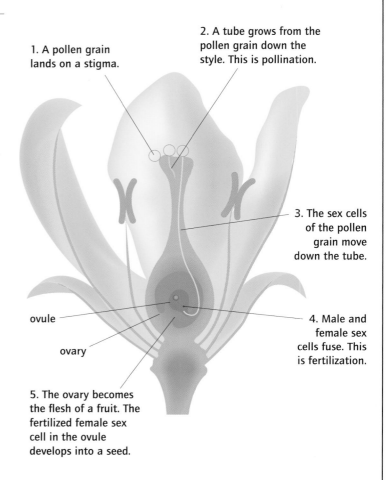

1. A pollen grain lands on a stigma.

2. A tube grows from the pollen grain down the style. This is pollination.

3. The sex cells of the pollen grain move down the tube.

4. Male and female sex cells fuse. This is fertilization.

ovule

ovary

5. The ovary becomes the flesh of a fruit. The fertilized female sex cell in the ovule develops into a seed.

Sex-cell production

The details of how sex cells are produced are complicated. Developing eggs in the ovary, for example, are surrounded by helper cells called nurse cells and follicle cells. These cells have various functions, including supplying the egg with nutrients. Egg cells, unlike sperm cells, often do not complete **meiosis** until the moment that a sperm fertilizes them. (Meiosis is the cell division that produces sex cells with half the number of chromosomes as body cells.)

Sperm are produced in the testes in a kind of production-line process, which involves not only meiosis but also the removal of most of the immature sperm cell's **cytoplasm** and the growth of its long flagellum. Other cells in the testes called Sertoli cells supply the sperm with nutrients. In most mammals the testes hang outside the main body cavity in a bag of skin called the scrotum. That is probably because sperm develop or keep best at a slightly lower temperature.

Getting together

Fertilization can be external (occurs outside the body) or internal (occurs inside the body, usually the female's). The release of eggs and sperm for external fertilization is called spawning. External fertilization is handy for many water-living organisms that cannot easily get together, such as corals or starfish.

Internal fertilization

Internal fertilization is vital for many land animals: First, because sperm cannot fly through air as they can swim through water, and second, in the case of birds and reptiles, because the eggs must be fertilized before the protective shells are added.

Internal fertilization is also vital for any females that keep the developing embryo inside their body. This applies not only to people and other mammals but also to sharks and many other animals. Usually the male has a structure (the penis in mammals) that places sperm in the female's body during mating, but some animals make use of waterproof packets of sperm, called **spermatophores**, instead.

Many animals, such as ostriches, engage in elaborate courtship displays. These are signals to the opposite sex that indicate an individual is ready to mate.

SCIENCE WORDS

- **cytoplasm** Contents of a cell outside the nucleus.
- **enzyme** Protein that speeds up chemical reactions inside an organism.
- **estrogen** The most important female sex hormone. It controls the development of sexual characteristics.
- **mate** When two individuals (the parents) come together to produce young.
- **meiosis** Process of cell division that produces sex cells.
- **ovary** Female gonad, which produces egg cells.
- **spermatophore** A packet of sperm in a protective coating that a male animal leaves somewhere for a female to pick up.
- **testosterone** The most important male sex hormone. It controls the development of sexual characteristics.

WHAT IS GENETICS?

What determines your height, hair color, ear shape, blood type, and every other feature of your body? The answer lies in your genes.

Everything about you, from the way you look to how your body functions, is controlled by genes. Genes are packets of information that form a code. You inherited your genes from your mom and dad. Genes occur on stretches of long chemicals called deoxyribonucleic acid, or DNA. Genetics is the study of how genes pass through the **generations** and the role of DNA and other chemicals.

Most cells in your body have a control center called a nucleus. The nucleus contains all the genes needed to make your body and keep it working.

An organism's complete set of genes is called its **genome**. DNA carrying the genes is organized into structures called chromosomes. Every species has a fixed number of chromosomes.

The importance of DNA
Genes are sequences of chemicals called bases on a very special molecule—DNA. Life as we know it could not exist without DNA. Genes on a DNA molecule work by driving the production of chemicals called proteins in the cell. Proteins may be products such as hormones. Proteins also include enzymes, without which chemical reactions inside the body could not take place. To make proteins using DNA, a similar chemical, ribonucleic acid (RNA), is needed.

Features such as this child's eye color depend on genes received from his mom and dad, although the environment in which he grows up will affect characteristics such as height and weight.

Inheriting alleles

Half of the 46 chromosomes inside each cell in your body are provided by your mom; the other half come from your dad. Male sex cells, or sperm, carry one set of chromosomes. Female sex cells, or eggs, carry the other. A sperm and an egg come together in a process called fertilization. That forms a cell called a **zygote**. You and everybody else started life as a zygote. The chromosome sets provided by your parents began to work together there. That's what makes you you.

The genes carried on the chromosomes tell your cells what color your eyes are and what size your nose is; every feature of your body is shaped by genes. Each feature, though, is coded for by two

Composed of sugars, phosphates, and chemicals called bases, DNA forms a twisted, coiled shape called a double helix (see page 27). Inside the nucleus DNA coils up very tightly and is bound with proteins to form X-shaped structures called chromosomes.

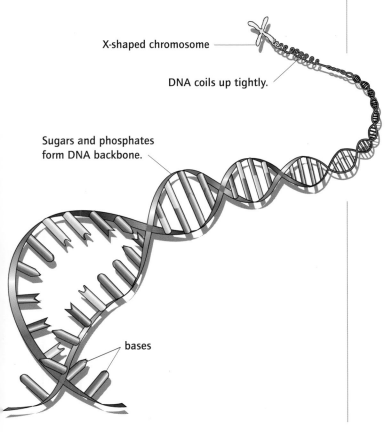

X-shaped chromosome

DNA coils up tightly.

Sugars and phosphates form DNA backbone.

bases

USING GENETIC KNOWLEDGE

Scientists use their knowledge of genetics to change the characteristics of organisms. Plants and animals can be selectively bred for useful features. In recent years crops and animals have been genetically modified (altered) to protect against pests or to increase yields. Genetically modified organisms are also useful in medicine, in the production of the hormone insulin, for example. Understanding inheritance helps physicians figure out the likelihood of genetic disorders such as hemophilia occurring.

Further advances have followed since the completion of the Human Genome Project (HGP) in April 2003. It saw the mapping of every human gene—an invaluable tool for medical researchers.

versions of a gene, one from your mother and one from your father. The paired genes are called **alleles**. Sometimes both alleles are the same, but different versions may be present. How does the body know which set of genetic instructions to follow?

The answer is that some alleles are dominant: The trait they code for is always shown when the alleles are present. Other alleles are recessive. Recessive alleles only come into effect in the absence of dominant alleles.

SCIENCE WORDS

- **allele** Any of the alternative forms of a gene that may occur at a given point on a chromosome.
- **genome** All the genes present inside an organism.
- **zygote** The fertilized egg created when an egg cell and a sperm fuse at conception.

THE PRINCIPLES OF INHERITANCE

Modern biologists' knowledge and understanding of inheritance, the way in which features pass from parents to their young, began with the findings of a 19th-century monk called Gregor Mendel.

Have you ever wondered why you look more like members of your family than your friends at school? Or why a cat never gives birth to a dog? The answers lie in the study of inheritance. Characteristics pass from parents to young in the form of genes. Scientists now know that genes are carried on stretches of deoxyribonucleic acid, or DNA, molecules.

The way characteristics move between generations is now well understood. But before the late 19th century inheritance was mysterious. The man who figured out how inheritance worked was an Austrian monk called Gregor Mendel (1822–1884).

Abbey experiments

Mendel carried out lots of experiments in the gardens of his abbey. He crossed (bred) different garden pea varieties. Eggs inside female flowers are fertilized by pollen, a powder that contains sex cells released by male flowers. Fertilized eggs develop into seeds. Using a fine brush to transfer the pollen, Mendel could cross two plants or make a plant self-pollinate (fertilize itself).

The diagram (opposite) shows what happened in one of Mendel's experiments. He crossed a pea with purple flowers with a white-flowered plant. The resulting seeds (called the **F1 generation**) were planted. All the young grew to have purple flowers.

Mendel then self-pollinated the F1 flowers. Of these young (the F2 generation) three-quarters had

Gregor Mendel chose to experiment with pea plants, such as the ones below, because characteristics such as flower color and seed shape were easy to identify and catalog.

COLOR CHANGES IN PEAS

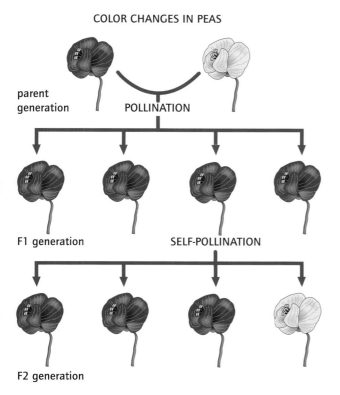

parent generation

POLLINATION

F1 generation

SELF-POLLINATION

F2 generation

This diagram shows what happened in one of Mendel's early experiments with pea plants. White flowers disappeared in the F1 pea generation, only to reappear in the F2 generation.

purple flowers. But one-quarter had white flowers, just like one of their grandparents. What on earth was going on?

Understanding the results

Mendel suggested that the particles responsible for passing on traits such as flower color occurred in pairs. One particle was contributed by each parent plant. Furthermore, he suggested that these particles separate from one another during the formation of sex cells (in this case the eggs and pollen). So each sex cell contained one particle. But the resulting young had two particles, since two sex cells fuse to form young. Mendel's inheritance particle is now called a gene. In the flower color experiment Mendel reasoned that the parent plants with purple flowers had two

similar versions of a gene—let's label them CC. The white-flowered plants had two different versions, cc. Each sex cell produced by the purple-flowered plant contained one C gene. Each sex cell produced by the white-flowered plant contained a single c gene.

The F1 generation received one gene from each parent. However, all the young plants had purple flowers. That was because the C gene masked the c gene. Biologists call these different forms of the same gene alleles. One allele, C, codes for purple flowers. The other, c, carries the code for white flowers. The C allele is always expressed when present and is referred to as dominant. By contrast, c is expressed only when C is absent and cannot mask its effect (here leading to white-flowered plants). Alleles like c are called recessive.

The F2 generation

All the F1 flowers are purple since their genotypes are all Cc. Take a look at the Punnett squares at the bottom of page 18 to see why. The F1 plants have an allele, c, that would lead to white flowers if the dominant C allele were absent. Each sex cell receives just one of the alleles—this is Mendel's first law, the Law of Segregation.

By crossing an F1 plant with itself, young with one of three genotypes are possible; CC, Cc, and cc. The Punnett square on page 18 shows why this is so. Three genotypes, but only two possible phenotypes: Since C masks c, CC and Cc produce the same result. Three-quarters of the F2 young have purple flowers; the rest have white ones.

Allele destinations

When a plant makes sex cells, do alleles from its mother go into one sex cell and those from its father go into another? Or can a single sex cell contain alleles from both mother and father? Mendel designed an experiment to find out. A diagram showing what happened is on page 19.

TRY THIS

How Do Punnett Squares Work?

Punnett squares give a simple way to figure out the **genotypes** of young, provided you know what the genotypes of the parents are. To fill in a Punnett square, take the genotype of the parents, and separate the alleles for each gene. That reflects the way alleles split in sex cell formation. Then write all the male sex cell alleles on one side of the Punnett square and all the female sex cell alleles on the other. Adding one to the other in the Punnett square gives all the possible genotypes of the young. This tells you what the young will look like, and in what proportions the resulting **phenotypes** are likely to occur.

Alleles pass randomly from each parent to the young. The Punnett square shows the allele combinations and in what proportions they occur. Here, three-quarters of the young are YY, and the rest are Yy.

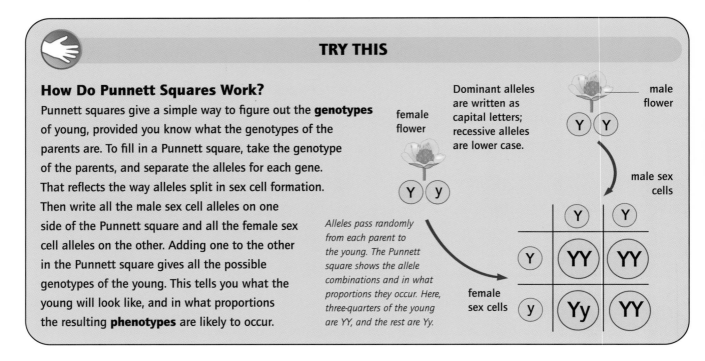

Dominant alleles are written as capital letters; recessive alleles are lower case.

Peas have genes for seed color and seed shape. Color has two alleles: Dominant Y, which produces yellow seeds, and y, which is recessive and leads to green seeds. Shape is also controlled by two alleles.

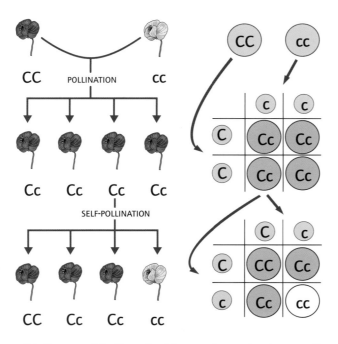

This diagram explains the results of the pea color experiment on page 17.

Dominant R produces round seeds, while recessive r produces wrinkled seeds.

In Mendel's experiment one parent produced round, yellow seeds (so its genotype was YY RR), and the other produced wrinkled, green seeds (yy rr). A cross between them produced F1 plants that were heterozygous for both genes—in other words, Yy Rr. The F1 plants had dominant alleles; they were yellow and round. Mendel then self-pollinated the F1 plants. If the alleles maintained the associations they had in the parent plants, then the F1 plants would produce sex cells with one of two types of genotypes—YR and yr. Then three-quarters of the F2 plants would have yellow, round seeds, and one-quarter would have green, wrinkled seeds. There would be no reason to suppose the traits were under the control of different genes since round seeds would always be yellow and wrinkled ones green.

However, this was not the case. The separation of Y from y and R from r in sex cell formation is independent. The F1 plants produce sex cells with four different genotypes in equal numbers. They are YR, yR, Yr, and yr. The Punnett square (opposite)

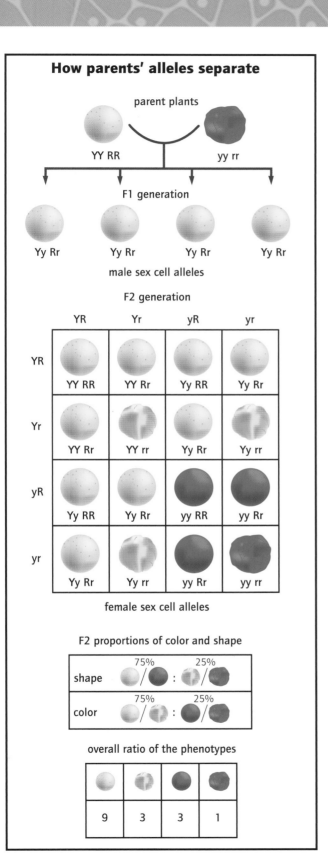

How parents' alleles separate

parent plants

YY RR   yy rr

F1 generation

Yy Rr   Yy Rr   Yy Rr   Yy Rr

male sex cell alleles

F2 generation

	YR	Yr	yR	yr
YR	YY RR	YY Rr	Yy RR	Yy Rr
Yr	YY Rr	YY rr	Yy Rr	Yy rr
yR	Yy RR	Yy Rr	yy RR	yy Rr
yr	Yy Rr	Yy rr	yy Rr	yy rr

female sex cell alleles

F2 proportions of color and shape

shape	75%	:	25%
color	75%	:	25%

overall ratio of the phenotypes

9	3	3	1

shows that there are nine possible combinations of genotypes in the F2 young. The young could have any one of three color genotypes (YY, Yy, or yy) and three possible shape genotypes (RR, Rr, or rr).

The F2 phenotypes

These combinations of genotypes yield four possible phenotypes. They include some combinations that did not appear in the original parent plants, such as yellow wrinkled seeds. The Punnett square enables us to predict how many of each phenotype appear in the F2 generation.

This experiment helped Mendel form his second law, the Law of Independent Assortment: Alleles of different genes separate independently in the formation of sex cells. There can be many different alleles for any one gene.

Lost and found

Mendel published his work in 1866. For around 40 years no one took much notice. Then other scientists rediscovered Mendel's research and used it to learn more about inheritance. Scientists found that genes occur within chromosomes, and that the genes themselves are formed by stretches of DNA molecules.

In 2003 geneticists completed the Human Genome Project, a map of all the genes of the human body. This incredible achievement could not have taken place without Mendel's work in the abbey gardens almost 150 years ago.

SCIENCE WORDS

- **F1 generation** The young produced by a pair of test organisms. The young of the F1 generation are called the F2 generation.
- **genotype** The genes in an organism that code for a certain phenotype.
- **phenotype** A feature coded for by a gene.

Growing, healing, and producing young: All these processes depend on the ability of cells to divide.

Cells are the body's building blocks. Every part of your body, from organs like your heart, liver, and stomach to tissues such as nerves and even your blood, contains cells. The function of each cell and how it develops are determined largely by the cell's DNA. DNA carries genes, a sequence of instructions telling the cell what to do. You inherited your genes from your parents.

Cells of living things such as animals and plants contain a control center, or nucleus, that houses the DNA. The nucleus is surrounded by a gel-like

This computer-generated artwork shows a human zygote at the eight-cell stage. The fertilized egg has divided three times by a process known as mitosis.

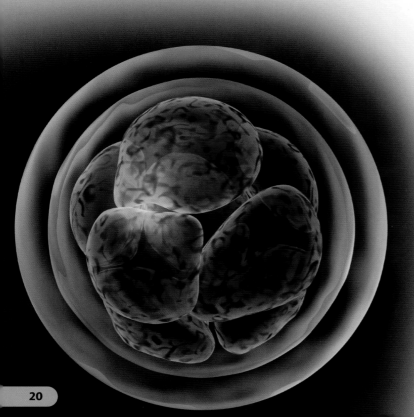

cytoplasm within which are various miniorgans, or **organelles**. All the contents of the cell are wrapped by a plasma membrane.

Cells have life cycles. A typical cell life cycle has two main stages. During the first of them, called interphase, the cell grows and produces proteins and other products. Body cells increase their numbers through a process called mitosis. This is the second stage in the cell life cycle. Cells multiply so dead cells can be replaced and the whole organism can grow. During mitosis a cell divides to produce a pair of new, or daughter, cells. However, each daughter cell needs a complete genome (all the genes in the body) for it to function properly. How do cells manage this feat?

Chromatin

Most cells in your body other than the sex cells contain two complete sets of DNA molecules. One set was provided by your mother, the other by your father. The two sets are very similar, but not identical. The DNA is packaged up with proteins in a complex mixture called chromatin. During interphase the chromatin in a body cell remains inside the nucleus, where it is strung out thinly and cannot be seen through a microscope.

What happens in mitosis?

Preparations for cell division are made during interphase. A pair of tiny rods called centrioles begin

The illustration below shows a typical animal body cell. The various parts inside, such as the mitochondria and nucleus, are "miniorgans" called organelles.

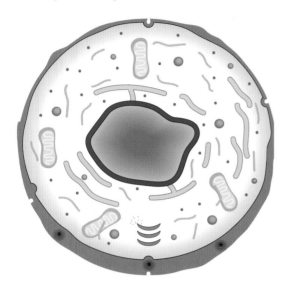

to replicate (copy themselves). Also, the cell's DNA replicates. This is an essential part of the process, since both of the cells produced by cell division need their own complete set of DNA.

Mitosis begins as the chromatin separates away from other proteins in the nucleus. The chromatin fibers shorten and thicken before coiling into sausage-shaped structures. They are called chromatids. Because the DNA in the cell replicated, there are two identical copies of each chromatid.

Identical pairs of chromatids link up to form X-shaped structures called chromosomes. The point in the middle of the X where the two chromatids join is called the centromere.

Setting up the spindle

Next, the two pairs of centrioles that formed during the cell's interphase move to opposite ends of the cell. A birdcage-like structure forms between the pairs. It is called the spindle. It acts as a kind of railroad track, controlling the way the chromosomes move. Meanwhile, the membrane that surrounds the nucleus, the nuclear envelope, begins to break down.

HOW MITOSIS WORKS

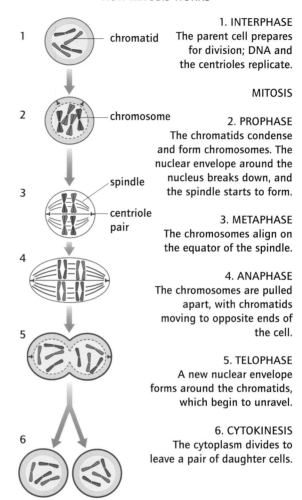

1 — chromatid

1. INTERPHASE
The parent cell prepares for division; DNA and the centrioles replicate.

2 — chromosome

MITOSIS

2. PROPHASE
The chromatids condense and form chromosomes. The nuclear envelope around the nucleus breaks down, and the spindle starts to form.

3 — spindle
— centriole pair

3. METAPHASE
The chromosomes align on the equator of the spindle.

4

4. ANAPHASE
The chromosomes are pulled apart, with chromatids moving to opposite ends of the cell.

5

5. TELOPHASE
A new nuclear envelope forms around the chromatids, which begin to unravel.

6

6. CYTOKINESIS
The cytoplasm divides to leave a pair of daughter cells.

PARTS OF A CHROMOSOME

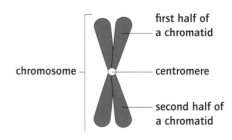

first half of a chromatid

chromosome — centromere

second half of a chromatid

Division takes place

The chromosomes begin to coil tighter and tighter. They line up along the equator, which is the middle of the spindle. The chromosomes attach at their centromeres to the spindle fibers. Then the cell and the spindle begin to stretch out. This pulls apart the identical chromatid pairs that form each chromosome. The chromatids move farther and farther along the spindle framework toward the centrioles, which lie at each end of the dividing cell.

The chromatids (or daughter chromosomes, as they are now called) reach the ends of the cell. A new nuclear envelope forms around each set of chromosomes. The chromosomes begin to unravel back into chromatin, and the spindle breaks down. All is now set for the physical division of one cell into two daughter cells.

Tiny filaments contract at the equator, narrowing the cell. The cell then splits into two daughter cells.

Both of the daughter cells contain a complete set of genes that is identical to that of the original cell.

Producing sex cells

Most of the cells inside your body are **diploid**. That means they contain two sets of chromosomes, one set is provided by your mother and the other set of chromosomes comes from your father, making up 46 chromosomes in total. Mitosis leads to the production of two daughter cells, each of which also has 46 chromosomes. But what happens when sex cells such as sperm and eggs fuse at fertilization?

If the sex cells were diploid, the resulting zygote (fertilized egg that develops into young) would have four copies of each chromosome—92 in total. The offspring of such a creature would have 184 chromosomes, and so on. To avoid this, sex cells need to be **haploid**—they must contain just one set of chromosomes. That ensures the zygote receives just the right number of chromosomes and no more.

Sperm and eggs are formed through a different type of cell division. Biologists call this type of cell division meiosis. The process of meiosis leads to the formation of haploid cells. For example, human

This illustration, below, explains the difference between diploid and haploid cells. Diploid cells contain two sets of chromosomes, but haploid cells have only one set of chromosomes.

1. Parent body cells are diploid. There are two sets of chromosomes, with 46 chromosomes in total.

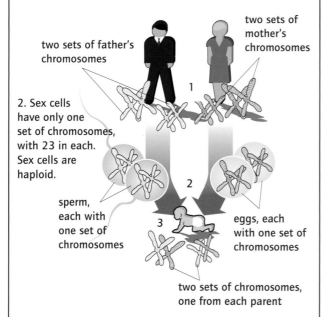

two sets of father's chromosomes

two sets of mother's chromosomes

2. Sex cells have only one set of chromosomes, with 23 in each. Sex cells are haploid.

sperm, each with one set of chromosomes

eggs, each with one set of chromosomes

two sets of chromosomes, one from each parent

3. Haploid sex cells fuse at fertilization. The baby produced has two sets of chromosomes, one from its mother and one from its father. So the baby is diploid like its parents.

WHEN DOES MEIOSIS TAKE PLACE?

Cells that divide to form sex cells have life cycles like any other cell, although such cycles can last for many years. If you are a girl, oogenesis—the process of egg formation—began before you were born. However, completion of meiosis is delayed until **puberty**, around age 13. From then on, meiosis continues, with one egg completing its development each month until you reach age 50 or thereabouts. If you are a boy, spermatogenesis, or the production of sperm, will not begin until you are around 14. The process of spermatogenesis will then continue for the rest of your life.

WHAT IS A KARYOTYPE?

A **karyotype** is an organized, visual profile of a person's chromosomes. Chromosomes are arranged and numbered by size, from largest to smallest, with the sex chromosomes last. To make a karyotype, a physician stains dividing cells to make the chromosomes visible and to add bands on them that match certain gene sequences. Then the physician takes an image and uses computer software to arrange the chromosomes according to size and banding patterns. That helps the physician quickly identify major chromosome disorders.

sperm and eggs contain 23 chromosomes rather than the 46 found in the nuclei of other body cells.

Why meiosis differs

Meiosis differs in another crucial way from mitosis. Mitosis is a mechanism for constancy. It ensures that the same set of genes appears in all the cells in the body. By contrast, meiosis promotes genetic

Eye color is an inherited trait, that is influenced by more than one gene. The gene combinations can produce colors ranging from brown (most common), through blue, to green (least common).

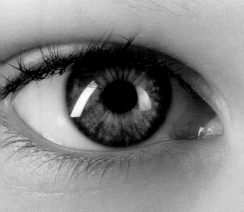

variation. The process leads to differences between the original DNA and that of the resulting sex cells.

A little variation between the generations is a good thing for organisms that reproduce sexually, such as humans. Variation can be acted on by natural selection, which helps organisms cope with changes in their environment. The diversity fostered by the process of meiosis explains why you look *similar* to your parents, brothers, and sisters, but not *identical* to them.

How meiosis happens

Meiosis causes cells to divide twice, although the cell's DNA only replicates once. The main objective of the first division is to promote genetic diversity. One-half of the 46 chromosomes inside each of your body cells is provided by your mother, with the other half provided by your father. Each pair of chromosomes is called a homologous pair, meaning they are similar in size and appearance (except the sex chromosomes, which might not match). Each chromosome in a homologous pair carries genes for the same traits, such as eye color. However, each chromosome may carry a different form, or allele, of that gene. One allele may lead to brown eyes, and the other might produce blue eyes.

Before meiosis can take place in your body, the cell must prepare for division. The DNA replicates, as

1. PROPHASE I
Chromatids join to form chromosomes. Matching pairs of chromosomes link up to form tetrads, and crossover may occur. The nuclear envelope breaks down, and the spindle forms.

1

2. METAPHASE I
The tetrads line up randomly on the spindle.

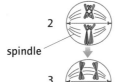

2

spindle

3. ANAPHASE I
The tetrads move to opposite ends of the cell.

3

4. TELOPHASE I
The chromosomes unravel, and nuclear envelopes re-form; the cells then physically divide.

4

5. PROPHASE II
The nuclear envelopes break down, and spindles begin to re-form.

5

6. METAPHASE II
The chromosomes line up along the spindle equator.

6

7. ANAPHASE II
The chromatids that form each chromosome are pulled apart.

7

8

9

8. TELOPHASE II
Nuclear envelopes re-form, and cells narrow at their equators.

9. CYTOKINESIS
The cells divide, leaving four haploid sex cells.

There are two cell divisions in meiosis, each with a set of stages. The name of each stage is followed by a number that explains which of the divisions is taking place.

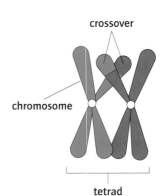

crossover

chromosome

tetrad

do the centrioles. As in mitosis, the chromatin fibers thicken, and identical pairs join at the centromere to form X-shaped chromosomes. But next the pairs of chromosomes join together to form structures called tetrads. One chromosome in a tetrad consists of two copies of the DNA code contributed by your dad. The other chromosome that makes up the tetrad is similar, but from your mom.

Gene swapping

The chromosomes forming the tetrads lie alongside each other. Corresponding genes on each match exactly. At this point the first process that will increase genetic diversity takes place. It is called crossover. Parts of each chromosome within a tetrad break at corresponding points, and chunks of DNA are then swapped. This random process mixes the DNA a person inherited from their mother and father.

Meanwhile, the nuclear envelope dissolves away, and a spindle forms that pushes the centriole pairs to opposite ends of the cell. The tetrads attach to the spindle and move to the equator. The way they line up there is random. Chromosomes provided by your mother or father may be on either side. The tetrads split, and the chromosomes are pulled to opposite ends of the cell. The cell then splits as in mitosis to leave a pair of daughter cells. The random way the tetrads align is the second source of genetic diversity; chromosomes from your mom or dad could end up in either daughter cell.

EXTRA CHROMOSOME SETS

Most plants and animals are diploid. Their genetic material includes two chromosome sets. Sometimes, offspring inherit more than two sets of chromosomes due to mistakes in meiosis. That is usually deadly for animals, but some plants can cope. Plants with extra chromosome sets are called **polyploids**. Many crops are polyploids. Sometimes the extra set comes from the same species. Bananas, for example, have three chromosome sets. That leads to large, seedless fruit. Bananas are sterile (cannot reproduce). New plants can only grow from cuttings.

Making eggs and sperm

Through crossover and the random alignment of tetrads on the spindle the daughter cells' DNA differs from the original DNA. Now the daughter cells divide again to form sex cells. This time the DNA does not replicate. The division process is similar to mitosis. Chromosomes align on a spindle before being pulled to opposite ends of each cell, which then divides.

When meiosis is complete, the one original cell has produced four sex cells. Each of these cells contains just one set of chromosomes—in other words, the cells are haploid. Each can now fuse with a sex cell from a mate to form a zygote.

Meiosis mistakes

Sometimes meiosis goes wrong. If chromosome pair 21 fails to separate from the tetrad, both may go to the same end of one of the daughter cells. The resulting eggs will have either two or no copies of this chromosome. Imagine that an egg with two copies of this chromosome is fertilized by a normal sperm. The zygote that forms has three copies of the chromosome. A child born with this extra copy is said to have Down syndrome.

SCIENCE WORDS

- **diploid** Cell or organism that contains two sets of chromosomes.
- **haploid** A cell such as a sex cell (or, rarely, the cells of a whole organism, such as a male ant) that contains one set of chromosomes.
- **karyotype** A visual profile of an organism's chromosomes, arranged in order of size.
- **organelle** Membrane-lined structures, such as the nucleus, inside eukaryote cells.
- **polyploid** Organism that contains more than two sets of chromosomes.

DNA AND RNA

The genetic material inside the cells of almost all living organisms is made of a chemical called DNA. A similar chemical, RNA, is important for producing proteins.

The key chemical in inheritance is called deoxyribonucleic acid, or DNA for short. A DNA molecule is shaped like a ladder that has been twisted around itself many times without breaking the rungs. This shape is called a **double helix**. The building blocks of DNA are called **nucleotides**. They are made of chemicals called phosphates as well as sugars. The sugars and phosphates form the "sides" of the DNA ladder.

Nucleotides also contain one of four other chemicals called bases. They are adenine (A), thymine (T), guanine (G), and cytosine (C). The bases form the ladder's "rungs." Bases on one side of the DNA ladder bind with bases on the other in a very specific way. Adenine in

one strand always forms a bond to thymine in the other, while guanine always bonds with cytosine.

Why is DNA so important?

In organisms such as animals and plants DNA occurs in the nuclei (control centers) of cells. DNA carries genes, which are sets of instructions formed by the order of the bases on the DNA molecule. Genes direct the production of a range of vital chemicals called proteins. There can be thousands of genes on any one DNA molecule, and each gene directs the production of a different protein. Some proteins help

This computer-generated artwork shows the double-helix structure of deoxyribonucleic acid (DNA), the molecule that lies at the heart of inheritance.

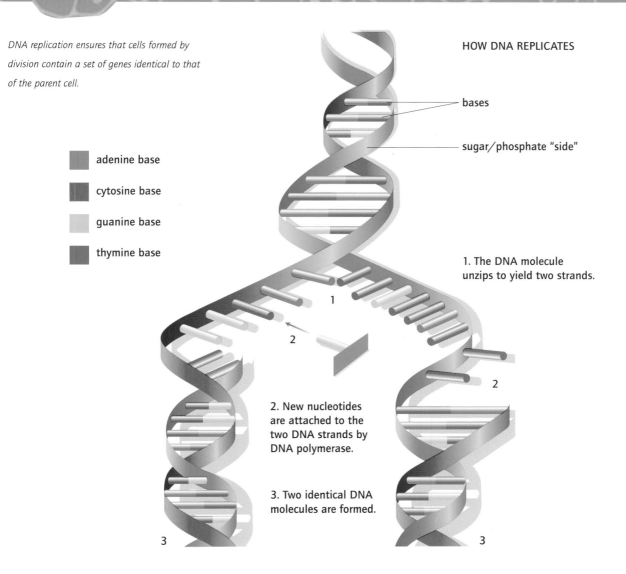

DNA replication ensures that cells formed by division contain a set of genes identical to that of the parent cell.

HOW DNA REPLICATES

bases

sugar/phosphate "side"

- adenine base
- cytosine base
- guanine base
- thymine base

1. The DNA molecule unzips to yield two strands.

2. New nucleotides are attached to the two DNA strands by DNA polymerase.

3. Two identical DNA molecules are formed.

form structures like tissues and organs. Others form cell products such as hormones.

Among the most important proteins are enzymes. They control the rate at which chemical reactions take place inside the body. Thousands of different chemical reactions occur inside a body cell. Some help make new cell products or parts; others are important for releasing energy or in cell division. None of these essential reactions could take place without the help of enzymes.

Proteins such as enzymes determine everything about an organism, from what it looks like to how its body parts function. That is why DNA is such an important molecule; without DNA proteins could not be made.

How DNA copies itself

With the exception of viruses, the process of cell division is essential for living creatures. Bacteria divide to produce more bacteria; cells inside animals and plants divide so the organism can grow and repair itself. But each new cell needs a complete set of genes to allow it to function properly. To ensure that happens, DNA molecules inside a cell that is about to divide go through a process of self-copying, or **replication**.

REPAIRING MISTAKES

DNA replicates with astonishing accuracy. Scientists have estimated that an error occurs in a gene only once in about one million cell divisions. How is the process so reliable? Many errors are removed by natural selection; the cell dies before it can divide. Other mistakes are corrected. A system of enzymes inside each cell scans DNA molecules after they have replicated. The enzymes then fix any mistakes in the base sequence.

Replication produces an exact copy of the DNA of the dividing cell. The first step in replication involves the uncoiling of the double helix. Each double-helix "ladder" then separates to form two strands. The paired bases that make up the "rungs" separate, and the two "sides" of the ladder unzip. Each strand will form a template for a new DNA double helix.

For the next step in the replication process an enzyme called DNA polymerase is needed. This enzyme helps nucleotides that are loose in the cell join to the strands. Molecules of adenine link to thymine, and molecules of guanine bond to cytosine.

HOW TRANSCRIPTION WORKS

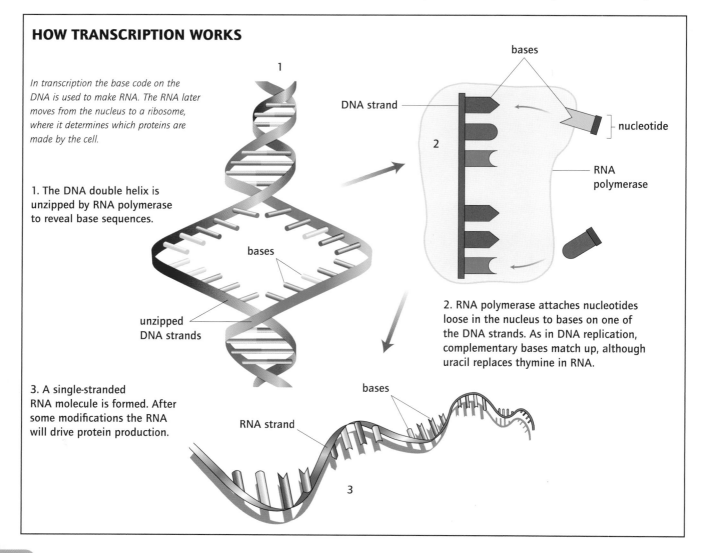

In transcription the base code on the DNA is used to make RNA. The RNA later moves from the nucleus to a ribosome, where it determines which proteins are made by the cell.

1. The DNA double helix is unzipped by RNA polymerase to reveal base sequences.

bases

DNA strand

nucleotide

RNA polymerase

bases

unzipped DNA strands

2. RNA polymerase attaches nucleotides loose in the nucleus to bases on one of the DNA strands. As in DNA replication, complementary bases match up, although uracil replaces thymine in RNA.

3. A single-stranded RNA molecule is formed. After some modifications the RNA will drive protein production.

bases

RNA strand

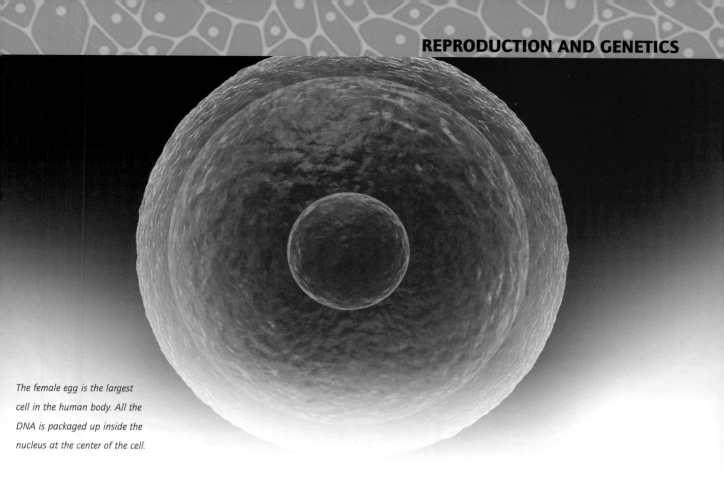

The female egg is the largest cell in the human body. All the DNA is packaged up inside the nucleus at the center of the cell.

The DNA polymerase moves along the template DNA strand, attaching the correct nucleotides as it goes.

The end result is two DNA molecules that are identical to the original version. Each consists of one new strand and one old one. The cell can now divide to produce two cells, each with a full complement of DNA.

DNA replication is essential for the growth of an organism and also for the inheritance of characteristics. Replication allows the genes of an individual to be carried in their sperm or eggs and passed on to the next generation.

What happens next?

Once a pair of new cells has formed following cell division, they get to work making proteins according to the instructions provided by the DNA. How does the DNA's sequence of bases control this process? To make proteins, another molecule, **ribonucleic acid (RNA)**, is needed. Like DNA, RNA is made up of nucleotides. The two chemicals are similar, although

RNA is smaller and occurs as a single strand rather than as a double helix.

RNA takes the code from DNA to the parts of the cell where proteins are made; it acts as an information carrier. RNA itself is made in a process called **transcription** (see opposite). First, an enzyme called RNA polymerase unzips part of the DNA double helix. That makes certain sequences of bases—the genes—accessible. One of the strands acts as a template in a way similar to DNA replication. The RNA polymerase moves along the strand, joining complementary nucleotides. This produces a strand of RNA. The RNA bears a sequence of nucleotides identical to that of the DNA strand that did not act as the template. The difference is that thymine is replaced in RNA by a fifth base type, uracil (U). Uracil binds only to adenine, as thymine does in DNA.

More enzymes swiftly go to work on the new RNA strand, sometimes even before transcription is complete. The enzymes add a sequence of bases at the end called the tail and a single base at the front called the cap. The tail and cap sequences protect the important parts of the RNA molecule from damage. Segments of the code called introns that play no part in protein production are removed. The finished product is called **messenger RNA (mRNA)**.

Producing proteins

Next, the sequence of bases on the mRNA molecule is used to make proteins. This process is called translation. The mRNA drifts from the nucleus into the cytoplasm (the part of the cell that lies outside the nucleus). There the mRNA's cap binds to a tiny organelle (miniorgan) called a **ribosome**. This is where the production of proteins takes place.

Biologists refer to the order of bases on the mRNA molecule as the triplet code. It is called that because a set of three bases (or triplet) codes for one

type of **amino acid**. There are 20 different amino acids that occur in organisms; they are the building blocks of proteins. The triplet code determines which amino acids join together where.

Meanwhile, different RNA molecules called **transfer RNA (tRNA)** bind to amino acids that are loose in the cell. Each tRNA molecule is formed by three nucleotides. The sequence of bases on the tRNA determines which type of amino acid it can join to.

From amino acid to protein

Complete with its amino acid luggage, a tRNA molecule with the correct sequence of nucleotides binds to an mRNA triplet. The ribosome holds the two RNA molecules in place. Another tRNA molecule plus amino acid then attaches to the next mRNA triplet along. That brings the two amino acids into

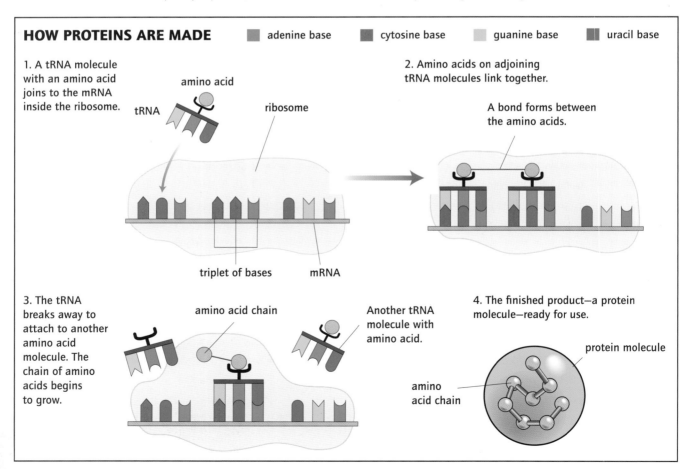

HOW PROTEINS ARE MADE ■ adenine base ■ cytosine base ■ guanine base ■ uracil base

1. A tRNA molecule with an amino acid joins to the mRNA inside the ribosome.

amino acid
tRNA
ribosome
triplet of bases
mRNA

2. Amino acids on adjoining tRNA molecules link together.

A bond forms between the amino acids.

3. The tRNA breaks away to attach to another amino acid molecule. The chain of amino acids begins to grow.

amino acid chain
Another tRNA molecule with amino acid.

4. The finished product—a protein molecule—ready for use.

protein molecule
amino acid chain

close contact. The ribosome joins the amino acids together before breaking the first tRNA free. The tRNA then floats away to bond with another amino acid (see diagram opposite).

The ribosome moves along the mRNA strand, repeating the process as it goes. The new protein molecule is now starting to take shape.

The chain of amino acids grows longer and longer. Eventually, the protein molecule is finished. It contains a sequence of amino acids that was determined by the triplets on the mRNA strand. They, in turn, were determined by the makeup of the DNA molecule back in the nucleus. The newly formed protein folds in a certain way before drifting off to carry out whatever function it is required for.

The control of genes

Although DNA molecules must replicate in their entirety before a cell divides, genes are not active in all of the cells all of the time. Any cell only has a limited number of functions in the body. For example, pituitary cells produce hormones that are not produced by any other body cells. There is control over which genes become active in any one cell and when. Regulator proteins are responsible for this control. They are enzymes that bind to the DNA a little way along from a target gene. Depending on the enzyme, they can either help or hinder the transcription of the gene. That allows genes to be switched on or off.

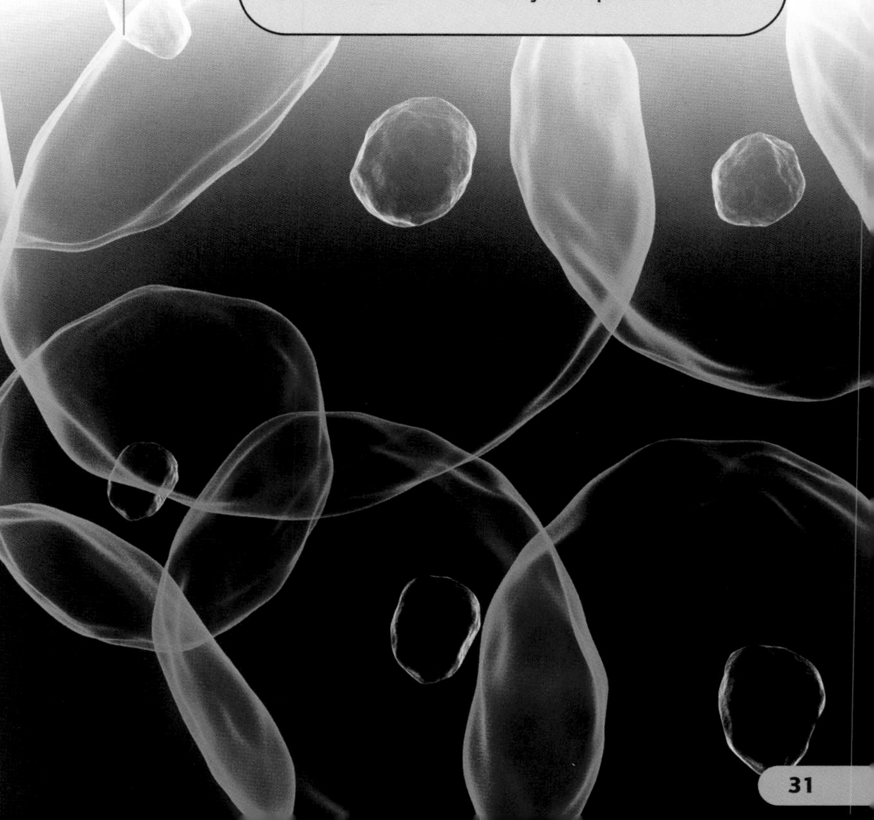

All the cells in an individual contain the same set of genes, but not all the genes are active in all of the cells. Sequences of DNA in the genome contain instructions to tell the cell how to switch genes on and off.

SCIENCE WORDS

- **amino acid** Nitrogen-containing molecule that is a building block of proteins.
- **double helix** Twisted ladderlike shape of a DNA molecule.
- **messenger RNA (mRNA)** Chemical that takes the genetic code from DNA in the nucleus to the ribosomes, where it becomes a template for protein production.
- **nucleotide** Part of a DNA molecule, comprising a sugar, a phosphate group, and a base.
- **replication** Self-copying of a DNA molecule.
- **ribonucleic acid (RNA)** Chemical similar to DNA involved in protein production.
- **ribosome** Granule on which protein production occurs.
- **transcription** The process of converting the coding sections of a DNA molecule into RNA.
- **transfer RNA (tRNA)** Type of RNA that binds to amino acids and brings them to a ribosome for assembly into proteins.

GENOMES

A single molecule of DNA carries units called genes that direct how the cell functions. Genes do this by controlling the production of proteins such as enzymes by the cell. The complete set of genetic material of an organism is called its genome.

The genome of a plant or animal may contain thousands of genes. DNA of these organisms occurs mainly in cell nuclei (control centers). Individuals of any one species have the same number of DNA molecules in each body cell's nucleus. Human body cells contain 46 DNA molecules. Before a cell divides, these molecules copy themselves. They then coil to form structures called chromosomes.

The entire set of chromosomes is called the karyotype. Scientists number the chromosome pairs within the karyotype in order of their size. In people the longest is pair 1, while pair 22 is the shortest. Pair 23, the sex chromosomes, is different. It has at least one very large (X) chromosome and may have one very small (Y) one. Each DNA molecule has a combination of genes along its length that does not change from one individual to another individual. So, for example, the gene that codes for the hormone insulin in people always occurs close to one end of chromosome 11. The position a gene occupies on a chromosome is called its locus (plural, loci).

How do genes interact?

The relationship between a gene and the characteristic it leads to is rarely simple. Some features are influenced by dozens of different genes. Often these characteristics do not follow simple patterns of inheritance. Height in people, for example, involves the interaction of many genes, as well as environmental factors. Some people are tall, others are short, while most are of average height. By contrast, there are only four blood groups—A, B, AB, and O.

Genes play an important part in determining the height of this basketball player, but environmental factors, such as diet, exercise, and sleep patterns, can also affect height and growth.

WHAT ARE LINKED GENES?

Some genes are said to be linked to others. Genes that lie on the same chromosome are considered linked, even though they code for different features. The genomes of plants and animals contain many such pairs. The genes for eye color and body color in fruit flies, for example, are linked (right). Linked genes may pass from parent to young together, unlike genes that lie on separate chromosomes. The closer together on a chromosome the genes lie, the more closely they are linked, and the likelier it is that they will be passed on together. Linked genes provide a good way to map genes positions on a chromosome.

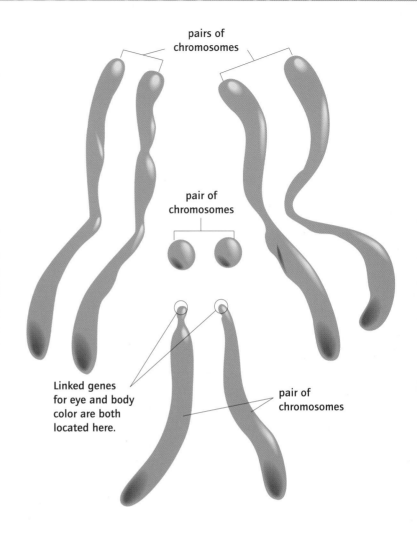

pairs of chromosomes

pair of chromosomes

Linked genes for eye and body color are both located here.

pair of chromosomes

Height is an example of continuous variation, with a large number of possibilities. Blood group is a type of discontinuous variation—a person can have only one of a fixed number of blood types.

Many genes control the function of others. They direct the production of enzymes that regulate the activities of other genes. The enzymes do so by clamping to key positions on the genome. In this way certain genes can stop others from working or switch them on.

Understanding genotypes

The genome consists of the gene sequences that occur at precisely defined loci on the chromosomes. But there may be one of several versions of each gene. These variants are called alleles. Alleles explain why you do not look identical to your friends or family. Humans have a variety of eye colors, for example, because there are several eye color alleles. Some combinations lead to blue eyes; others lead to brown, green, or gray eyes.

The combination of alleles in an individual is called the genotype. Every cell inside you carries the

Fruit flies have four pairs of chromosomes. Genes for different traits that occur on any one chromosome are linked.

same combinations of alleles—they all share the same genotype. That is because each body cell is the product of countless numbers of cell divisions starting from the fertilized egg in your mom's **uterus**. Each time a cell divides, the DNA inside replicates, keeping the genotype the same in every cell. The precise nature of your genotype depends on the alleles carried by the sperm and the egg that fused to make you.

How many sets?

Matching chromosomes have genes that code for the same features at exactly the same loci. So, for example, there are two copies of the insulin gene in each human body cell because there are two copies of chromosome number 11.

For most animals body cells, such as those of the liver, skin, or heart, carry these double chromosome sets. Cells like these are called diploid. When eggs or sperm form during the process of cell division called meiosis, these sets separate into different daughter cells. Sperm and eggs carry a single copy of each of the chromosomes: These cells are called haploid cells. When sperm fertilizes an egg, the resulting cell (or zygote) has two chromosome sets—it is diploid, just like the body cells of the animal into which the zygote develops.

Not all organisms are diploid. In an ant colony, for example, female worker ants and the queen ant are diploid, but the males are haploid. Many types of plants, as well as some other organisms, have more than two sets of chromosomes in their cells. These organisms are called polyploids.

Mapping genomes

Biologists began to decode the entire genomes of animals in the 1980s. Early research programs looked at the genomes of bacteria and other tiny organisms. Later, small animals such as fruit flies and roundworms were

TORTOISESHELL CATS

Can you find a male tortoiseshell cat? You might have some problems. A gene on a cat's X chromosome determines the tortoiseshell coat, which is characterized by black, cream, and brown markings. Two different alleles are involved. They are "black" and "yellow." Tortoiseshell cats have both alleles, which means they must have two X chromosomes. That means they must be female. Male cats have only one X chromosome, so they cannot have a tortoiseshell coat.

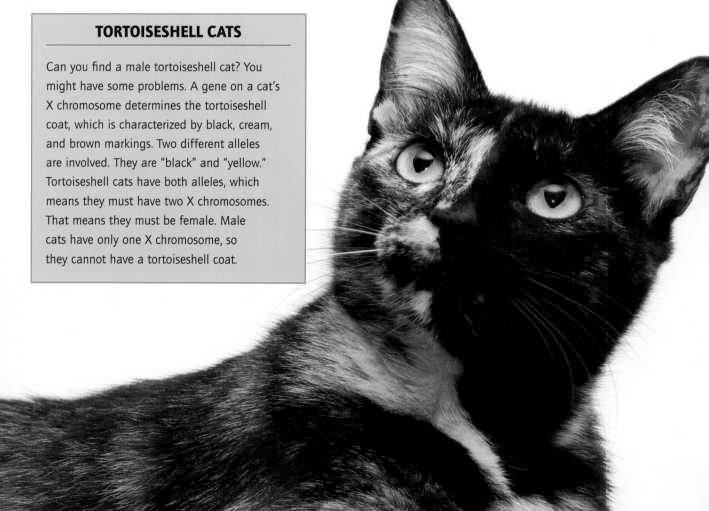

THE SOCIAL LIFE OF ANTS

Ants are social insects that live in colonies. All the young are produced by one ant, the queen, which mated with a male before founding the nest. The worker ants do not lay eggs, but still manage to get their genes into the next generation. How do they manage this?

All depends on the unusual nature of ant genetics. Queen and worker ants are diploid, with two sets of chromosomes. Males, however, are haploid—they only have one chromosome set. As with humans and other diploids, the queen shares half her genes with her young. But each daughter—worker or new queen—shares, on average, three-quarters of her genes with the other daughters. So bizarrely, more of a worker ant's genes pass to the next generation if she does not breed. Instead, it pays for a worker to tend to the queen and help her produce more of the worker's sisters.

In a worker ant's ideal world all the young produced would be new queens. But the queen needs workers to feed and look after her and the young. So she releases chemicals that control whether a young female ant becomes a queen or a worker. That keeps the numbers of each at the right level.

studied. The greatest achievement in this field to date was the completion of the Human Genome Project (HGP) in 2003. The HGP has led to dramatic advances in our understanding of various diseases. Doctors can now offer genetic tests to show predisposition to a variety of illnesses, such as breast cancer, cystic fibrosis, liver diseases, and many more. Since the completion of the HGP, the genomes of other animals have been studied.

SCIENCE WORDS

- **uterus** A stretchy muscular sac in female mammals within which embryos develop.

Worker ants share three-quarters of their genes with the offspring of the colony queen. By tending to the offspring they are ensuring their own genes are passed on to the new generation. This behavior is known as altruism.

HUMAN GENETICS

Human chromosomes carry the genetic code. Genes drives cell development, but some can cause inherited diseases.

DNA, in the form of genes, directs the way that every cell in your body functions. Genes are inherited by children from their parents. The complete set of genes in a body cell is your genome. After many years of work scientists completed the Human Genome Project, or HGP, in 2003. That involved mapping the entire human genome. The HGP had important implications for treating genetic disorders.

The human genome

Every species of living organism has a certain number of chromosomes. They carry genes that form a code that determines the physical characteristics of the organism. Chromosomes are formed by coiled-up molecules of DNA. The number of chromosomes varies among species. Humans, for example, have

Slight differences in the human genome are enough to create people with different appearances. This genetic variation is the result of slight differences in the sequence of DNA.

46 chromosomes, fruit flies have just 8, while one type of fern has 1,260!

Of the 46 human chromosomes, 44 can be arranged into pairs of similar size and structure; they are called homologous (matching) pairs. The remaining pair are called the sex chromosomes. One of your sex chromosomes was provided by your mother and is called an X chromosome. The other member of this chromosome pair was provided by your father. It may be another X or a different, smaller chromosome that carries few genes, called a Y. If you are a girl, you received a pair of X chromosomes from your parents. If you are a boy, you got one X and one Y chromosome.

This arrangement of sex chromosomes has important implications for the inheritance of certain diseases. That is because many inherited diseases are linked to the X chromosome.

Inside the sex cells

The nucleus (control center) of most human cells contains a full set of 46 chromosomes. Cells with this full complement of chromosomes are known as diploid. Things are different in the sex cells—sperm in men and eggs in women. These cells are produced by a type of cell division called meiosis.

Meiosis leads to cells with 23 chromosomes, half as many as other cells in the body. Cells like these are called haploid cells. They become diploid again only if fertilization occurs.

Fertilization happens when a sperm penetrates an egg. Then the two haploid cells join, producing a cell called a zygote that has the full set of 46 chromosomes. This new diploid cell divides again and again to form an embryo. The embryo develops further and eventually grows into a baby.

Natural clones

Although everyone has the same types of genes, no two people look exactly the same. That is because genes have variants (different forms) called alleles.

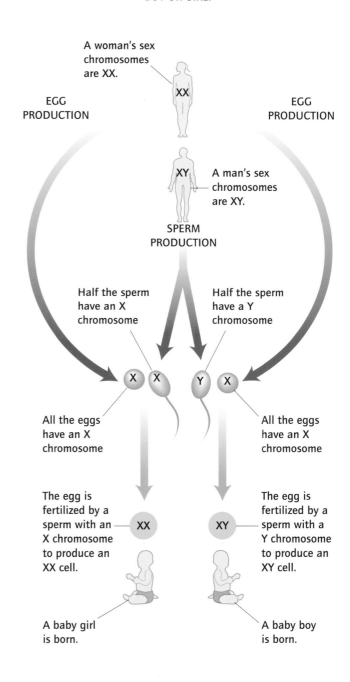

BOY OR GIRL?

A woman's sex chromosomes are XX.

XX

EGG PRODUCTION

EGG PRODUCTION

XY — A man's sex chromosomes are XY.

SPERM PRODUCTION

Half the sperm have an X chromosome

Half the sperm have a Y chromosome

X X   Y X

All the eggs have an X chromosome

All the eggs have an X chromosome

The egg is fertilized by a sperm with an X chromosome to produce an XX cell.

XX

The egg is fertilized by a sperm with a Y chromosome to produce an XY cell.

XY

A baby girl is born.

A baby boy is born.

A person's sex depends on the combination of sex chromosomes received from his or her parents. When sperm are formed inside a man, some are X and others Y. Chance alone decides which type fertilizes a woman's egg.

Even most twins do not look alike. Identical twins are the only exception to this rule. In this case a single sperm fertilizes an egg, just as in single births. However, the fertilized egg splits in two early in its development. This leads to two **fetuses** growing in the uterus rather than one. The resulting pair of babies are clones: They are genetically identical.

TRY THIS

Color Blindness

Take a look at this picture. What do you see? You can probably see the number 8 in bright red, surrounded by darker red dots. However, if you are color blind, you will be unable to make out the number. This is called an Ishihara test. It is a good way to find out if a child is color blind. Color blindness is caused by a recessive sex-linked allele. Women can act as carriers for this allele. To suffer from the disorder, a woman must inherit two copies of the recessive allele—a rare event. Men, on the other hand, are far more likely to be sufferers. They do not have a second X chromosome on which a dominant allele can occur.

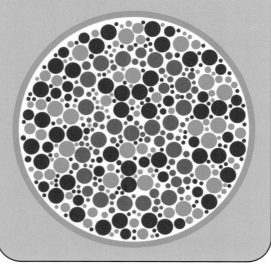

Allele combinations

Everybody has a unique combination of alleles. It is called a person's genotype. You inherited your genotype from your parents. Whether you have a feature of one parent or the other depends on the types of alleles you received from them.

Alleles come in two forms. Dominant alleles are always expressed regardless of what the other allele is. Recessive alleles are different. A recessive allele is expressed only if two copies of it are present; in other words, in the absence of a dominant allele. For example, the allele for brown eyes (B) is dominant. It masks the effect of the recessive allele for blue eyes (b). Similarly, the allele for brown hair (H) is dominant, while the fair hair allele is recessive (h).

Features of a child also depend on the allele combinations of their parents. Sometimes both alleles of a gene are identical. They are called homozygous alleles. Different alleles in a pair are called heterozygous alleles.

Imagine a man who is homozygous for both brown hair and blue eyes (HHbb). His wife is homozygous for fair hair and brown eyes (hhBB). All their children will have brown hair and brown eyes because the alleles that code for these characteristics are dominant. However, all the children will be heterozygous for these features—in other words, their genotype will be HhBb. That is because they will have inherited recessive alleles for fair hair and blue eyes (h and b) as well as the dominant varieties (H and B) that are expressed.

Sex-linked traits

Genes that are carried by the sex chromosomes are called sex-linked genes. You might think that characteristics more common in men are the result of genes that lie on the Y chromosome. However, the Y chromosome has very few genes; instead, sex-linked genes are usually present on the X chromosome. Conditions such as hemophilia (a disorder of the blood) and color blindness are sex-linked traits. These conditions are caused by recessive alleles. Women are carriers—they pass on a condition but only rarely have it themselves. That is because women have a second X chromosome that usually contains a dominant, healthy allele. It masks the effects of the recessive version.

Men are much more likely to suffer from a sex-linked disorder than women are. The Y chromosome does not provide a dominant allele to compensate for a recessive allele on the X chromosome.

Inheritance of disease

In the late 1890s British physician Archibald Garrod (1857–1936) suggested that genetic defects caused inherited diseases. Disease can also be caused by poor diet or infectious organisms, but about 4,000 diseases are the result of inherited disorders.

Some genetic diseases, such as cystic fibrosis, are caused when recessive alleles are inherited from both parents. Cystic fibrosis causes, among other symptoms, serious breathing difficulties. The gene responsible occurs on chromosome 7. A disorder called Tay-Sachs disease is caused by the body's failure to produce a key brain protein, leading to death at around age 4. Most common in children of European Jewish ancestry, Tay-Sachs disease is caused by a **mutation** to a gene on chromosome 15.

Chromosome abnormalities

Some genetic diseases are not inherited but are caused by problems with the number of chromosomes present. Down syndrome is caused by the presence of an extra copy of chromosome 21. People with this condition have 47 chromosomes in their cells rather than the usual 46. Sufferers of Klinefelter's syndrome have more sex chromosomes than normal. Instead of having two sex chromosomes (XX or XY), sufferers have three—they can be XXY or XYY. People with another disorder, Turner's syndrome, have only one sex chromosome (XO).

Scientists are using the DNA found in fossil remains to trace the evolutionary origins of human beings.

SCIENCE WORDS

- **fetus** Unborn animal that is more developed than an embryo. In people the embryo becomes a fetus eight weeks after conception.
- **mutation** A change in a cell's DNA.

LIFE CYCLES

An organism's life cycle is the series of changes it undergoes from birth to the production of the next generation of organisms that are of the same type as the individual at the cycle's start.

To reproduce successfully, it is not enough just to give birth, lay eggs, or release seeds. At least some offspring need to survive to adulthood and reproduce successfully in turn.

Some organisms, such as people and all other mammals, complete their life cycle in one generation. The young grow up and produce the same type of young they were as infants. Some organisms complete their life cycle in two distinct phases, the gametophyte and sporophyte. The gametophyte form of the plant produces sex cells which combine to produce the sporophyte form of the plant. This method of reproduction is known as alternation of generations.

Infinite variety

Scientists trying to classify the life-cycle patterns of organisms have an uphill task. Animals, plants, and other living things show an amazing range of life spans and a variety of life histories. Individual bacteria, for example, can have a life cycle of as little as 20 minutes. That is the time between one cell division and the next. By contrast, certain trees, such as sequoias, can live for hundreds of years. Some living things, such as octopuses, mayflies, and bamboo plants, reproduce only once in their lives and then die. There are animals and plants that rely entirely on sexual reproduction, others that only reproduce asexually, and some that use a mixture of the two. Many life-forms have young stages that are completely different from the adults.

As a first step to understanding this complexity, scientists sometimes contrast two different kinds of life-history strategies. They point out that among plants many common weeds put most of their effort into producing seeds, not tough, long-lasting bodies for themselves.

Adult mayflies live for only a few days and die after mating, but their larvae live underwater for much longer.

EGG OR EGG CELL

A complication when discussing eggs is that shelled eggs and egg cells are not the same thing, although both develop into offspring. In a bird or reptile egg the egg cell becomes the embryo (developing animal). The outer layers (the egg "white" and the shell) are secreted by the mother's body before the egg is laid. The white and the shell protect the growing embryo.

The egg's yolk is a huge single cell packed with food supplies. Once fertilized, an egg divides and develops into a chick or reptile. Farmed hen's eggs are unfertilized, which is why you do not find baby birds in eggs you eat.

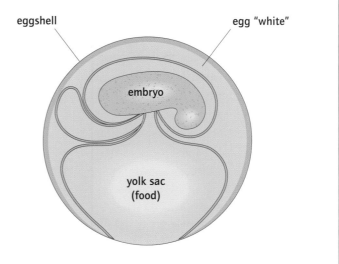

This illustration shows the shelled egg of a typical reptile.

These weeds both grow and reproduce quickly, soon spreading in favorable conditions (such as on newly cleared bare ground). By contrast, most trees do not become sexually mature for several years. Instead, many grow large, sturdy bodies that dominate their habitat and survive everything except major disasters. The weeds and the trees have different strategies, but both can be successful under the right conditions. Not all living things fit neatly into these categories, though; many fall between the two extremes.

A good start

A vital factor in the success of an individual animal or plant is the help it gets from its parent(s) at the start of life. From the offspring's point of view the more help they get, the better. For parents, though, it sometimes pays to concentrate on producing more offspring, even if each one gets less assistance.

Eggs, embryos, and seeds

There are many different ways of giving the next generation a good start in life. River-living animals often glue their eggs to stones and plants to keep them from being swept away. Many insect mothers lay their eggs on the plants or even inside other animals that their young later eat. Turtles bury their eggs for safety, crocodiles guard theirs until they hatch, and spiders wrap theirs in cocoons. Plant seeds can be tiny, with hardly any stored food (such as many orchids), or they can be giant food supplies like the coconut.

Evolution of eggs

Among vertebrates (backboned animals) the development of eggs with shells was a huge leap forward because it enabled the entire life cycle to take place on land. By contrast, amphibians such as frogs generally have to return to water to breed. This limits the types of places amphibians can live in.

Shelled eggs first evolved in reptiles. All dinosaurs probably laid eggs. Birds inherited their egg-laying ability from their dinosaur ancestors. Among mammals only a few species such as the platypus still lay eggs.

Parental care

A lizard or a snake hatches from its egg looking much like a small adult. It needs no help from its

CHEATS AND HOSTS

Some animals do not take care of their young after they hatch but still give their offspring a good start in life. Certain animals have figured out how to trick or use other animals (called hosts) into feeding or sheltering their offspring (1). If the host is harmed, then the relationship is parasitic. Some parasites kill their hosts; they are called parasitoids (2).

1. Eggplant lace bugs lay eggs that they guard until hatching time. Some females sneakily lay their eggs with another female's eggs. The sneak then leaves the other female to guard both sets of eggs.

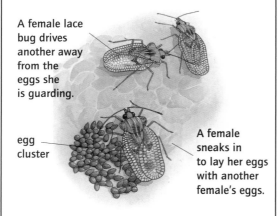

A female lace bug drives another away from the eggs she is guarding.

egg cluster

A female sneaks in to lay her eggs with another female's eggs.

2. Female parasitic wasps have a long egg-laying tube called an ovipositor. This one is using her ovipositor to inject an egg inside a beetle larva (grub). The ovipositor can pierce bark. When the wasp's egg hatches, the wasp larva feeds on the beetle grub, eating it from the inside out.

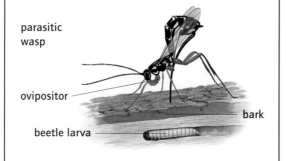

parasitic wasp

ovipositor

bark

beetle larva

parents and starts hunting for food immediately. By contrast, the young of many other animals, especially birds and mammals, need a lot of care from their parents to grow up and survive to breed.

Some species of mammals produce young that start life in a relatively advanced state, for example, deer, ducks, and ostriches. The young of grazing animals such as antelope can generally run soon after birth. Otherwise they would soon fall victim to predators. Other species of birds and mammals produce young in a more helpless condition, for example, cats, mice, humans, prairie dogs, and small songbirds.

One advantage of parental care is that it helps the young survive until they are big enough to keep warm by themselves. Birds and mammals are both warm-blooded; their body temperature is controlled internally. In birds both parents usually look after the young. Mammals vary, but for most species it is only the mother that provides parental care. That is because mammalian mothers nurse their young on milk from mammary glands.

LIFE STAGES OF A HOUSEFLY

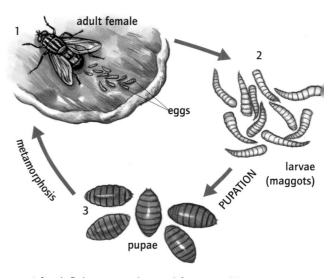

adult female

eggs

larvae (maggots)

PUPATION

pupae

metamorphosis

A female fly lays eggs, perhaps on left-out meat (1). Larvae (maggots; 2) hatch from the eggs. The larvae feed until they are ready for adulthood. They then go through a pupal stage (3), during which they metamorphose into adults.

THE ULTIMATE SACRIFICE

Many animals and plants do not (or hardly) survive after producing young. Adult salmon swim up rivers to reproduce and then die, exhausted. Octopuses (right) guard and tend their eggs until they hatch but do not feed and starve to death. After guarding their eggs, some female spiders allow the young to eat their own body—the ultimate in self-sacrifice.

Some male anglerfish attach themselves to a female, then literally become another part of her body. The male's nonbreeding structures degenerate (waste away), and he remains attached to the female for the rest of his life. You might wonder why such creatures bother to reproduce at all. It is because although the parent either degenerates or dies, its genes are passed on to the next generation. (Genes are inherited units of information carried by DNA.)

Invertebrate carers

Most invertebrates (animals without backbones) produce so many eggs that some are bound to survive and develop into adults. After releasing their eggs, most invertebrate parents leave the young to look after themselves. A few invertebrates, however, do practice parental care: Crayfish carry their young around for protection, a few bromeliad crabs house and feed their young, and some carrion-eating beetles feed their young grubs from their mouths. The champion invertebrate carers are social insects such as ants, termites, and some bees and wasps. The grubs of these insects are fed and looked after not by their mother (the queen) but by their older, nonbreeding sisters.

Life stages

Many animals produce young stages called larvae, which are different from their parents. The larvae of insects, for example, are often noticeably different from the adults or other **life stages**. Adults and larvae live and feed on different types of foods and so look different too.

When scientists first examined these creatures under a microscope, they had no idea that some of the tiny weird-shaped animals they saw were the larvae of crabs, sea urchins, or clams. They thought the creatures were new species and gave them their own names, such as zoea. Some of these names are still used as convenient labels for larval types, but they are no longer official scientific names.

Seafloor animals such as clams, starfish, and crabs often produce millions of tiny larvae that feed themselves on plankton. Plankton is all the life-forms that float in the surface waters of the oceans. Among the plankton there is also a supply of tiny algae and other particles that even the very smallest planktonic larvae can eat.

Invertebrates living in freshwaters tend to use an alternative strategy, producing fewer but larger eggs with more yolk in each. This is an advantage for life-forms living in running water, where smaller

UNUSUAL LIFE CYCLES

We are used to the idea of adult parents having several children, but how about the opposite—one child giving rise to many adults? That is what happens in the life cycle of many parasitic worms, including the liver flukes that infect humans. These creatures produce eggs sexually, which then hatch and go through several larval stages, often infecting different hosts such as snails. Some larval stages form asexual structures inside themselves, so a single larva gives rise to many of the next kind of larva. In this way thousands of adults can result from only one egg. A similar process happens in jellyfish.

Adult jellyfish (medusae; 1) reproduce sexually. Their eggs (2) hatch into planulae (swimming larvae; 3) that settle on the seabed and grow into small, sea anemone-like animals (4). As they grow, these polyps split into slices (5). Each slice is a young jellyfish, or ephyra (6), produced by asexual budding.

The ephyrae break free and develop into medusae. This process is often called "alternation of generations," but it differs from the alternation of generations in plants. That is because there is no genetic difference between the life stages of a jellyfish.

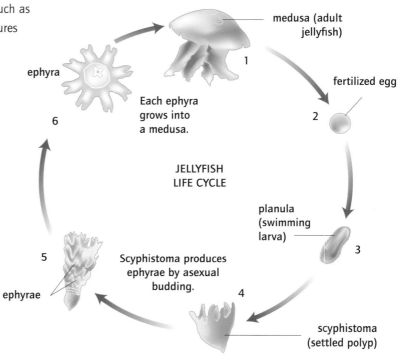

JELLYFISH LIFE CYCLE

1 — medusa (adult jellyfish)

2 — fertilized egg

3 — planula (swimming larva)

4 — scyphistoma (settled polyp)

Scyphistoma produces ephyrae by asexual budding.

5 — ephyrae

6 — ephyra

Each ephyra grows into a medusa.

eggs and tiny larvae would be swept away. The eggs of freshwater snails, for example, generally hatch into miniature adults, skipping the larval stage altogether.

Differences between life stages also help ensure that young and adults are not in competition for the same food or home.

From stage to stage

In insects there are two main patterns of growth. Some, including butterflies, beetles, ants, and flies, have a grublike larval stage that eventually turns into a nonfeeding pupa. Adult tissues grow inside the pupa. Other insects such as cockroaches reach their adult form more gradually. Any major change in shape, such as from a maggot to a fly, is called metamorphosis. The process involves much of the original larval tissue being broken down.

In frog and toad tadpoles adult development is promoted by thyroid hormone. In insects, by contrast, adult development is prevented by a hormone called juvenile hormone. When this hormone is eventually switched off, adulthood can be reached. Metamorphosis is a vulnerable time, so animals often hide away while it happens or make the process quick.

In mammals and birds life stages are usually not so distinct. Juveniles, though, are often differently patterned than adults. That might keep adults from seeing them as rivals or potential mates. The age of first breeding varies hugely, from a few weeks in mice to up to 15 years in albatrosses, for example. Primates (monkeys, apes, including humans, and their relatives), with their big brains and complex social structures, take much longer to reach adulthood than other mammals of the same size.

Seasonal cycles

Life and reproductive cycles are often linked to the seasons, especially in temperate (cooler) climates, where animals and plants have to cope with winter.

PEDOMORPHISM

Some animals never fully grow up but keep some or all of the features they had as larval stages all through their adult lives. This is called pedomorphism, meaning "of a childlike form." Classic examples are species of salamanders such as the mudpuppy and the axolotl. Most amphibians begin life as aquatic larvae. The larvae **metamorphose** (change) into land-living adults. Axolotls never change but keep the feathery gills that enable them to live in water as both larva and adult.

The axolotl retains some of the features of the larva, such as the feathery gills, and lives in water throughout its adult life.

Many temperate insects, for example, take a year to reproduce, while in the tropics they could complete their life cycle in a few weeks. That is because they sit out the winter in a sleeplike state called diapause. Among butterflies there are species that spend the winter as eggs, others as caterpillars, pupae, or adults. In other words, there is no single "best" life stage in which to overwinter. Even so, overwintering as an adult or juvenile is relatively rare. Most temperate insects spend the winter as pupae or eggs. These life stages require no food, which is scarcer in winter months. In North America monarch butterflies migrate hundreds of miles south each fall to avoid harsh northern winters.

Some animals manage several generations per year even in cooler climates, but only reproduce sexually as winter approaches. The rest of the time

BIOLOGICAL CLOCKS

Many living things have internal rhythms or "biological clocks" that match natural cycles such as day and night, and time of year. The rhythms are not absolutely exact but can be adjusted or "reset" by information coming from the outside. Changes in day length, for example, act as a guide to what time of year it is. The amount of sunlight and day length can affect phenomena from breeding cycles to emotional states. Biological clocks involve various genes that regulate each other's activities in a rhythmical way, and scientists are still figuring out the full details. Land organisms' clocks are generally geared to the day and the time of year, but sea creatures work to these and other rhythms, including the cycles of the moon and tides.

they might breed asexually, which increases their numbers quickly. Even species that survive several years usually time their reproduction to the seasons. Generally their young are born in spring, when there is plenty of food. There are exceptions, however. One is Eleanora's falcon, which lays eggs that hatch in fall—the parents feed their chicks on migrating songbirds that are common at that time of year.

Winter and summer are not usually so extreme in the sea, but seasons are important. That is because most sea animals fertilize their eggs externally. For a species living in a certain area it helps greatly if all individuals release their sex cells on the same days of the year. The timing of this can be astonishingly accurate. In the Great Barrier Reef, Australia, a few days after November's full moon most of the corals release their sex cells at the same time. Spawning at the same time as other members of the same species is a good move for sexual animals that cannot move around to find a mate.

MONARCH LIFE CYCLE

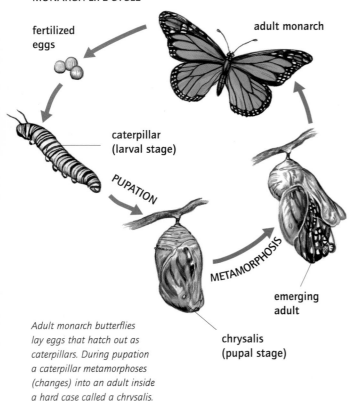

fertilized eggs

adult monarch

caterpillar (larval stage)

PUPATION

METAMORPHOSIS

emerging adult

chrysalis (pupal stage)

Adult monarch butterflies lay eggs that hatch out as caterpillars. During pupation a caterpillar metamorphoses (changes) into an adult inside a hard case called a chrysalis.

Species dispersal

Life stages are important in dispersing (spreading) species to new habitats. Among sea creatures, floating eggs and larvae (young) often do most of the spreading. This is especially the case if the adults are slow movers. Baby spiders can spread by spinning long silk threads that catch in the wind. In insects the winged adults are the main dispersal stage.

Seeds and fruits of plants have many different adaptations to aid dispersal. Sometimes dispersal is a disadvantage. Insects on remote islands often evolve to be flightless, and that can help prevent them being blown out to sea. Some desert plants produce large flat seeds that cannot blow away. That ensures the seeds remain in what might be the only place with water for miles around.

Corals use many reproductive strategies. Some species release millions of eggs and sperm cells, often in precisely timed mass-spawning events. This strategy allows the stationary corals to mix up their genes and to disperse over great distances.

SCIENCE WORDS

- **life stage** Distinct stage in an organism's life cycle. Larvae (young) such as caterpillars, tadpoles, fish fry, fly maggots, and beetle grubs are life stages. In mammals, birds, and reptiles the two main life stages (juvenile and adult) are less distinct.
- **metamorphose** To change physical form, especially when going from one life stage to another.

HUMAN REPRODUCTION

Humans are sexual animals. The purpose of sex is to bring together a sperm (male sex cell) with an egg (a female sex cell). When this occurs, the resulting fertilized cell, or zygote, develops into a new person.

With very rare exceptions, every person is born either male or female. Each child has primary sexual characteristics; a male has a penis, a female has a vagina. Other sexual characteristics develop later. When children near their early teens, their bodies begin to develop secondary sexual characteristics: facial and chest hair on boys, breasts and wider hips on girls, and pubic hair on boys and girls. These secondary sexual characteristics develop as the body prepares itself for reproduction and reaches sexual maturity during a life stage called puberty.

Women have all their sexual organs located inside the body. As well as internal sexual organs, men have two external sexual organs: the penis and the testes. A man's penis serves to penetrate a woman's vagina and deliver sperm to the vicinity of her uterus, where it can fertilize an egg. The testes (singular, testis) produce sperm.

Fertilization takes place when a sperm cell fuses with an egg. The fertilized egg, or zygote, will undergo cell division and develop into an embryo.

FEMALE REPRODUCTIVE SYSTEM

A woman's eggs are produced in the ovaries, which are on each side of the abdomen. A baby girl is born with all the eggs she will ever have. The eggs do not become active until later in life, though.

The ovaries also produce the female sex hormone, estrogen. Hormones are messenger chemicals released by glands that control long-term body functions. Among other things, estrogen causes female secondary sexual characteristics, such as breasts, to develop.

Fallopian tubes connect the ovaries to the uterus (or womb). When a women is pregnant, the baby develops inside the uterus, which is a stretchy, muscular sac. At the base of the uterus is the cervix, which opens when a baby is about to be born. The vagina connects the uterus to the outside of the body.

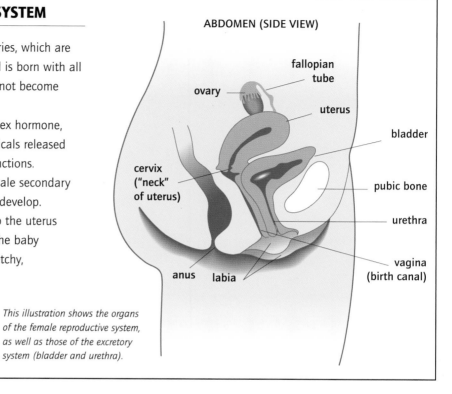

ABDOMEN (SIDE VIEW)

fallopian tube
ovary
uterus
bladder
cervix ("neck" of uterus)
pubic bone
urethra
vagina (birth canal)
anus   labia

This illustration shows the organs of the female reproductive system, as well as those of the excretory system (bladder and urethra).

Menstruation

Girls are born with all the eggs—about 750,000—they will ever have. When a girl reaches puberty, her ovaries begin pumping out estrogen and other hormones, such as progesterone. The girl's body begins to mature sexually.

At this time **menstruation** begins. Every 28 days or so one of her ovaries releases a mature egg in a process called **ovulation**. The egg moves into one of the fallopian tubes. At this time the lining of the uterus (the endometrium) prepares for a possible pregnancy by enriching itself with blood. If the egg is not fertilized, after about 10 days the enriched surface of the uterus breaks down. Some of the endometrial cells and blood, as well as the unfertilized egg, are expelled from the body during the woman's menstrual period. Menstruation lasts, on average, three to five days. The timing and length of menstruation is controlled by estrogen and progesterone produced by the ovaries.

Conception

Conception occurs when a sperm fertilizes (fuses with) an egg. The fertilized cell then develops into a baby. Conception only occurs when a woman is ovulating, and the egg is within a fallopian tube. Men ejaculate (release) about 300 million sperm during sex. Each tadpolelike sperm swims madly up the vagina, heading through the cervix ("neck" of the uterus) to the egg waiting in the fallopian tube. Most sperm fail at their one and only goal since only one sperm can fertilize an egg.

Pregnancy to birth

A woman's egg is fertilized while it is still in a fallopian tube. From there the fertilized egg travels to the uterus, where the egg embeds itself in the wall of the uterus.

A fertilized egg is called a zygote. While the zygote travels through the fallopian tube, it begins to divide, creating more cells. When it is a solid ball of cells, called a morula, the zygote enters the

MALE REPRODUCTIVE SYSTEM

A man's sperm cells are produced in the testes (or testicles), which are located in a sac called the scrotum. Unlike women, who are born with all their sex cells, men continually produce sperm throughout their adult lives. There is a good reason why the testes are outside the male body: Sperm develop only at a lower temperature (95–97°F; 35–36°C) than normal body temperature (98.6°F; 37°C).

The testes also produce the male hormone testosterone. This chemical messenger leads to the development of male secondary sexual characteristics such as facial hair and a deeper voice. From the testes immature sperm travel to a tube, called the epididymis, in the testes, where they remain for about 20 days until they mature. Before they are released, the sperm are mixed with a nutrient-rich, milky liquid called seminal fluid, which is made in the prostate gland. Seminal fluid reaches the testes through a long tube called the vas deferens. This mixture of sperm and seminal fluid is called semen.

Semen is released from the body through the penis, which is made of soft, spongy, tissue. The penis stiffens when a man is sexually aroused, or gets an erection. During sex the semen travels through the man's urethra to leave the body through the penis. Nature has given the male urethra a dual role: as a channel for urine leaving the body and as a channel for semen leaving the body.

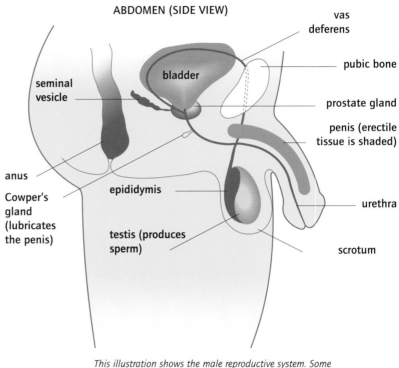

ABDOMEN (SIDE VIEW)

vas deferens

pubic bone

bladder

seminal vesicle

prostate gland

penis (erectile tissue is shaded)

anus

Cowper's gland (lubricates the penis)

epididymis

urethra

testis (produces sperm)

scrotum

This illustration shows the male reproductive system. Some excretory structures (bladder and urethra) are also included. The epididymis, vas deferens, and urethra form the sperm canal. The seminal vesicle and prostate produce seminal fluid.

uterus. By the time it is implanted in the endometrium, it has many cells and is called a blastocyst. It takes about a week for the zygote to reach the uterus and implant itself in the uterine lining, or endometrium.

Developing, unborn baby

Once the zygote is firmly implanted, the endometrium develops a thick, blood-filled layer that nourishes the developing zygote. A disk-shaped **placenta** develops in the uterus. The placenta is made up of tissue from both the developing zygote and the mother. It is filled with blood vessels that are attached to both and allows the baby to use the mother's circulating blood, from which the baby obtains oxygen and necessary nutrients. Placental blood also carries waste, such as carbon dioxide, away from the baby's cells and out through the mother's body. The placenta is expelled soon after childbirth. Childbirth occurs after a gestation, or

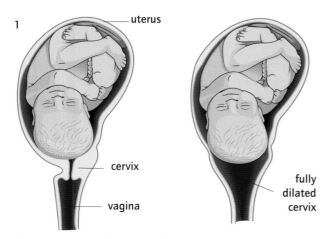

uterus

cervix

vagina

fully dilated cervix

1. The baby has reached full term and is head down, ready to be born. The cervix dilates (opens) to 4 inches (10 cm).

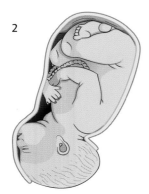

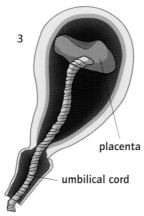

placenta

umbilical cord

2. The mother and her uterus push the baby out past the cervix and through the vagina.

3. The placenta is delivered.

development, period of 275–280 days. That is about nine months.

Labor and delivery

Labor is a series of powerful and painful contractions of the uterus. The muscular contractions help open the cervix. This makes a passage for the baby through the birth canal (vagina) and out of the body. The first signs of labor are brief contractions. Often the amniotic sac within which the baby lies also ruptures, and amniotic fluid flows out of the vagina. Though each labor and delivery is different, some basic stages occur:

1. During the first—and longest—stage contractions become increasingly frequent, longer, and stronger. The cervix opens to 4 inches (10 cm), while contractions are up to 90 seconds long each and occur every few minutes.
2. The second stage of labor begins when the cervix is completely open and delivery of the baby occurs. This is also called the pushing stage, since the woman pushes the baby out. Stage two lasts from 3 minutes to 2 hours.
3. In the third stage the mother expels the placenta and umbilical cord (a tissue that connected the fetus's abdomen to the mother's placenta) from her body. This stage usually lasts just a few minutes but can be longer.

Sexual health

Infertility Sometimes couples want to have a child, but the man or the woman might be infertile (physically unable to have children). There are many reasons why someone might be infertile. A woman will be infertile if, for example, her fallopian tubes are blocked due to infection, surgery, or a sexually transmitted infection. Or she may have or have had endometriosis, in which the endometrium is damaged and cannot support an embryo.

Men will be infertile if they produce too few sperm. A man's sperm count is considered low if he produces fewer than 50,000,000 sperm in every milliliter (ml) of semen. Low sperm counts can be caused by physical blockages or other abnormalities. Certain human-made chemicals can also affect sperm counts.

Sexually transmitted infections (STIs) Sex is a great way for infectious bacteria and viruses to ensure that they are passed on from one host to another.

Most sexually transmitted infections (STIs) have similar initial symptoms: pain, burning sensations, discharges, blisters, or sores. However, people can be infected with viruses that cause AIDS or genital herpes and yet still appear perfectly healthy, without

INFERTILITY TREATMENTS

There are an increasing number of high-tech methods to treat or help people overcome infertility. Among them are:

- **In vitro fertilization (IVF)** In IVF women are given drugs that stimulate production of mature eggs (1). Ultrasound is used to monitor the eggs as they ripen (2). The eggs are removed (3) and combined with sperm (4). The embryos that result are placed in an incubator, where they develop. At a certain stage the embryos are inserted into the woman's uterus (5), where normal development can occur. IVF often leads to multiple births.

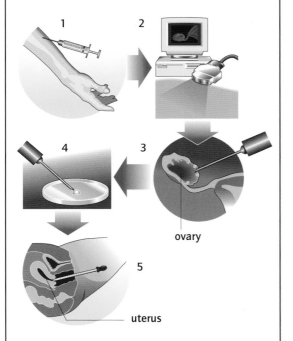

ovary

uterus

- **Sperm aspiration** Sperm are surgically removed from the testes of men who cannot produce sperm in their semen. The sperm are then injected into a woman's mature eggs or can be frozen for future use.

any of these symptoms. Some STIs, such as syphilis and chlamydia, can cause infertility. Syphilis can eventually lead to heart disease, central nervous system damage, and death. Chlamydia is a common STI that has hardly any noticeable symptoms, yet it can cause infertility in women. Many bacterial STIs can now be treated with antibiotics. But bacteria, including those that cause a common STI called gonorrhea, are becoming resistant to antibiotics.

Genital herpes is a common STI for which there is no cure. The virus that causes genital herpes is related to but not the same as the herpes virus that causes cold sores; it can only be passed on during sexual contact. Genital herpes is forever; once you get this viral infection, you cannot get rid of it.

HIV/AIDS

HIV (human immunodeficiency virus) is an STI in a class by itself. HIV destroys the body's immune system by infecting its cells. When first contracted, HIV has flulike symptoms, which disappear in a few weeks. For the next 7 to 10 years the virus is in its so-called chronic stage, when the infected person has no symptoms, but the virus is most often spread via unprotected sex (sex without a condom). During its chronic stage the virus is in constant battle with the immune system. Drug treatment can slow the course of the disease, but there is currently no cure or vaccine available.

When the immune system is defeated, the infected person has full-blown AIDS (acquired immune deficiency syndrome). His or her immune system is in ruins, and he or she will die, not of AIDS but of some other infection that the immune system cannot fight. HIV is spread though body fluids such as blood, semen, and vaginal secretions. It can spread through sexual activity if a condom is not used.

CONTRACEPTION

MALE CONDOM: A rubber sheath that fits over the penis and prevents sperm from entering the vagina.

MALE PILL: Chemicals taken orally or by injection inhibit sperm production.

MALE STERILIZATION: The vas deferens can be cut and (or) tied, preventing the release of sperm.

FEMALE STERILIZATION: The fallopian tubes are cut and (or) tied to prevent eggs reaching the uterus.

THE PILL: Some pills interfere with the release of eggs (ovulation); others affect the lining of the uterus, making it inhospitable to fertilized eggs or making the cervical mucus too thick for sperm to penetrate.

FEMALE CONDOM: A female condom lines the inside of the vagina, preventing sperm from entering the uterus.

CAP AND DIAPHRAGM: A cap or a diaphragm is worn over the cervix to prevent sperm entering the uterus.

IUDs: Intrauterine devices stop fertilized eggs implanting in the uterus.

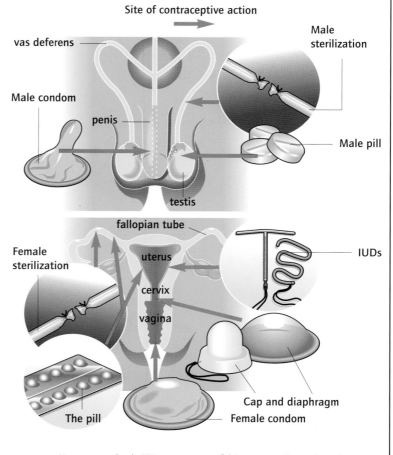

No contraception is 100-percent successful. In women who smoke or have other risk factors, the pill could cause serious side effects. Only condoms protect against sexually transmitted diseases as well as pregnancy.

An estimated 60 million Americans carry this virus. Antiviral drugs help relieve symptoms but cannot destroy the infection. In adults the symptoms are outbreaks of painful sores on the genitals. In newborns, who can catch genital herpes from their mother during birth, the disease might cause mental retardation or blindness. In the worst case scenario, the disease may even result in death.

The bugs that carry STIs are transmitted via sexual fluids during intercourse. So, if a man or woman uses a condom during sex, the likelihood of getting or transmitting an STI is greatly reduced.

SCIENCE WORDS

- **menstruation** Period during which a female mammal discharges blood and sheds the thickened uterine lining. Only occurs in the absence of pregnancy.
- **ovulation** The periodic release of unfertilized eggs in female animals, including people.
- **placenta** A blood-rich temporary organ in the uterus during pregnancy. It nourishes the embryo. People and some fish, such as sharks, have placentas.

Everyone begins life as a single cell—a fertilized egg—that develops into a fully formed person. As people grown older, the mind and body change.

After a woman's egg is fertilized by a man's sperm, the single-celled fertilized egg, or zygote, begins to divide. Ordinary cell division, or mitosis, continues until the zygote is made up of about 16 cells. By this

This portrait shows three generations of people within the same family. Children grow rapidly from birth, but this development slows down as children become adults.

point the zygote has traveled to the uterus, where it continues to develop. By day five or six the zygote is made up of many identical cells.

Differentiation

One week after fertilization the zygote's cells begin to differentiate: The cells develop differences from one another that will enable various tissues to form, such as muscle, bone, and blood. Differentiation is controlled by genes, which are units of inherited information in every cell.

When differentiation starts, the cells begin to form three layers (see opposite): the endoderm, which becomes the lining of the lungs, digestive

FROM ZYGOTE TO EMBRYO TO FETUS

A father's sperm and a mother's egg fuse and form a zygote (fertilized egg; 1). The zygote becomes a solid ball of cells called a morula (2), which enters the uterus. A cavity develops inside the morula, and it becomes a blastocyst (3). Its inner cell mass will develop into an embryo. At day five or six, when the cells start to differentiate, a "fold," or cleavage, appears in the embryo. Around the same time, the blastocyst implants in the uterine wall (4). By days 17 to 19 the ectoderm has thickened and formed a neural plate at the site of the former cleavage. This plate develops into the spinal cord and brain. By day 19 the embryo looks like the sole of a shoe when viewed from the top (5). The head is at the wider end. At 48 days the embryo begins to attain the features it will have after birth, so it is now called a fetus (6). The fetus grows from the head downward, with the brain developing early, and the hands developing before the feet. At nine weeks the fetus is about 1.25 inches (2.85 cm) long, and it has fingers. By 12 weeks the fetus can lift its hand to its mouth and suck its thumb. At seven months the fetus begins to put on fat in preparation for its life on the outside. After 9 months the baby is born.

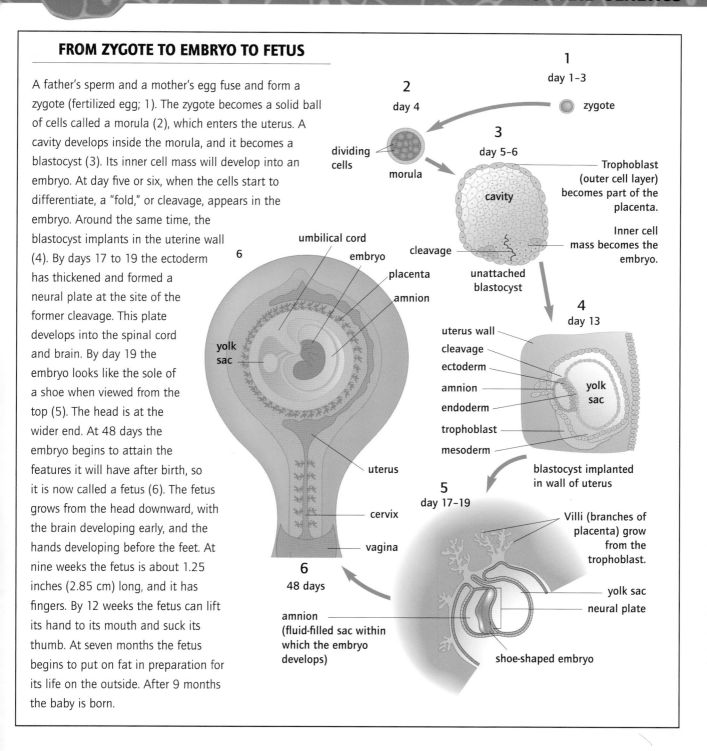

1
day 1–3
zygote

2
day 4
dividing cells
morula

3
day 5–6
cavity
Trophoblast (outer cell layer) becomes part of the placenta.
Inner cell mass becomes the embryo.
cleavage
unattached blastocyst

4
day 13
uterus wall
cleavage
ectoderm
amnion
endoderm
trophoblast
mesoderm
yolk sac
blastocyst implanted in wall of uterus

5
day 17–19
Villi (branches of placenta) grow from the trophoblast.
yolk sac
neural plate
shoe-shaped embryo

6
48 days
umbilical cord
embryo
placenta
amnion
yolk sac
uterus
cervix
vagina
amnion (fluid-filled sac within which the embryo develops)

tract, and other organs; the mesoderm, which forms the muscles, bones, blood, heart, and other organs; and the ectoderm, which forms, among other things, the skin, nails, hair, and nervous system.

Genetic switches

The genes you inherited from your parents determine many of your physical characteristics, such as eye and hair color. Genes are segments of

STEM-CELL RESEARCH

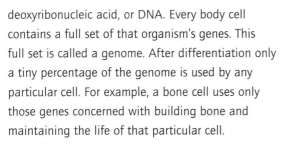

Until they differentiate, cells can become any type of cell since they contain a full set of genes. This ability is called totipotency. Totipotent cells are called stem cells (right) since all other cells stem from them. Scientists are learning how stem cells can be used to create new organs for people. Stem-cell research, and the healthy body parts it could yield, is one of the most promising but controversial fields of medical research.

Human stem cells come from fertilized human eggs. Some people believe that using unborn people for medical purposes is unethical.

If the stem cells came from places other than embryos, however, ethical problems may be resolved: Researchers have discovered that stem cells from umbilical cords can differentiate into nerve cells. Also scientists have recently created a stem-cell line. These are cells grown in a laboratory that can reproduce indefinitely.

deoxyribonucleic acid, or DNA. Every body cell contains a full set of that organism's genes. This full set is called a genome. After differentiation only a tiny percentage of the genome is used by any particular cell. For example, a bone cell uses only those genes concerned with building bone and maintaining the life of that particular cell.

Biologists have figured out that there must be genes that function as switches to turn "on" some genes (such as those related to bone building) and turn "off" others (such as those a bone cell does not need). Homeobox genes, which control differentiation in embryos, were discovered in the 1980s. Other genes regulate the timing and rate at which you grow after birth.

Stem-cell research has revealed an amazing 918 genes that regulate embryo development. Of them 254 had never before been recognized as acting on the embryo. The 918 genes are being studied to determine what they regulate.

Growth

Growth involves physical and psychological (emotional and mental) changes. In its first six months of life a child's growth is usually measured by physical changes in its body.

Newborn to infant During its first month of life a baby is considered a newborn. Most newborn behavior involves reflexes, especially sucking. Reflexes occur with no conscious effort. Newborn babies grow rapidly. At two months the brain and nervous system are developed enough for the newborn to start controlling some of its own movements. Basic motor skills develop from the top down: first, turning and lifting the head, last, control of the legs and feet.

Infant growth slows at about three months; by five months most babies are twice their birth weight. Between the ages of 6 and 12 months infants begin teething, take a first step, use their first two-syllable sounds. During the same period infants begin to display definite and individual personalities.

Childhood The four stages of childhood are based on major psychological developments: toddler, preschooler, early school years, and preteen. In toddlers (one to three years old) language develops rapidly, and motor skills are refined. Toddlers begin to achieve a sense of self. They might realize, for example, that they are a separate person from their main carer. During the so-called "terrible twos" toddlers are apt to respond "no" to almost any parental request. Most children begin to walk and are toilet trained during this stage.

Preschoolers continue to develop language and social skills. They play with others and learn to share. Their basic motor skills improve; and as their nervous systems develop, they attain greater fine motor skills, such as the ability to draw with a pencil.

The early school years are a time of physical growth, but also of major social and psychological development. Between the ages of five and eight children become socialized: They learn acceptable standards of behavior and how to better interact with people and the world around them. Schoolchildren become more independent and begin to solve problems. They recognize differences and determine

Between the ages of six and nine months, most babies are able to sit up without any help from their parents. Babies then learn to crawl as they try to explore the world around them.

their own preferences. During this time children form a self-image. This self-image is affected by the attitude toward them of others, particularly parents.

The preteen years, between the ages of 8 and 12, are a time of rapid physical growth and often the onset of puberty (physical sexual development). Preteens crave independence and are often under peer pressure to conform.

The physiology of growth

Height is the primary measure of growth, since it reveals the development of just one tissue, bone. People grow most quickly in the uterus, with the rate reaching a peak when the fetus is about 34 weeks old. People grow in a controlled and balanced way, though different body tissues grow at different rates and at different times. After a fetus reaches about 12–16 weeks, different people grow at different rates.

Growth glands All human growth is controlled by glands of the endocrine system. Glands are tissues that produce hormone. Hormones are molecules that control or trigger chemical reactions in the body. Some hormones are concerned solely with growth. The glands that produce growth hormones are the pituitary gland (controlled by the hypothalamus), the thyroid, the adrenal glands, and the sex organs.

The hormones produced by the pituitary and thyroid glands ensure steady growth patterns; so, for example, both your legs are the same length. Hormones produced by the adrenal glands and the gonads work differently. They cause abrupt and dramatic changes in the body's growth pattern.

GLANDS AND HORMONES

The main controller of growth is the hypothalamus. This gland lies deep within the brain. The hypothalamus ensures brain cells work properly and determines the timing of various stages of growth, such as the start of puberty. The hypothalamus seems to be an internal clock that knows when the body is ready for growth.

At a signal from the hypothalamus the pituitary gland at the base of the brain is activated. The pituitary's anterior (front) lobe is the headquarters for growth control. That is why it is often called the body's master gland. The pituitary gland produces pituitary growth hormone, or PGH. PGH is vital for children's growth. It stimulates the thyroid gland, which releases its hormones on orders from the pituitary. Thyroid hormones control the development and maintain the proportions of many of the body's organs. The thyroid hormone thyroxine works with PGH to ensure bones grow.

At puberty the hypothalamus signals the pituitary to secrete large quantities of hormones called gonadotrophins. Gonadotrophins act on the sex organs: They stimulate a young man's testes and a young woman's ovaries to begin producing their respective sex hormones (testosterone in men and estrogen in women).

In boys the adrenal glands produce hormones called androgens that work with testosterone to stimulate the growth and body changes associated with sexual maturity. In girls it is the hypothalamus that stimulates the ovaries to produce estrogen, and that triggers menstruation. Adrenal androgens function less in adolescent girls than in adolescent boys.

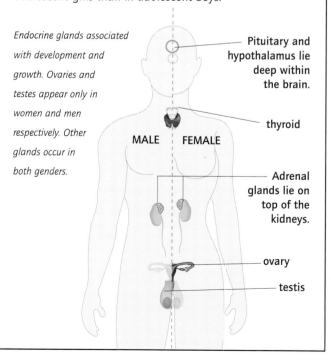

Endocrine glands associated with development and growth. Ovaries and testes appear only in women and men respectively. Other glands occur in both genders.

MALE | FEMALE

Pituitary and hypothalamus lie deep within the brain.

thyroid

Adrenal glands lie on top of the kidneys.

ovary

testis

As children grow into adults, they do not rely on as much parental support and start to take responsibility for their own actions.

The adolescent spurt Adolescence starts at puberty, which begins between the ages of 11 and 14 and lasts for approximately 6 to 10 years. Several hormones cause the dramatic growth and changes associated with adolescence. The spurt begins with growth of arms and legs; the head gets longer and straighter in profile. Many adolescents are keenly aware of the changes in their skin, which becomes coarser as oil-producing glands become active (sometimes causing acne).

Puberty produces secondary sex characteristics. Hormones cause boys to grow facial and chest hair, to develop deeper voices and stronger muscles. Girls develop breasts and wider hips. Both boys and girls grow pubic hair. As puberty goes on to maturity, the proportions of the adult body are set, and the hormones that raged in adolescence stabilize.

Growing older

Aging is the process of growing old. It is evident in people, since in many places the average length of life, or life expectancy, now extends far beyond the time when people tend to have children.

It is becoming increasingly important for scientists to understand how and why the human body ages. That is because the population in places such as the United States, Europe, and Japan is growing older. The care of people with age-related medical conditions costs billions each year. We need to discover how to maintain health well into old age.

ARTHRITIS

As people get older, they become less agile since their joints become stiff and are sometimes painful after years of wear and tear. Affected joints include the knees, hips, hands, feet, and shoulders. This condition is called **arthritis**. Nearly everyone develops some degree of arthritis by the age of 70.

As people get older, the skin becomes wrinkled and the hair turns gray. Some people suffer from mental deterioration such as memory loss.

Life expectancy and aging in people

The average life expectancy for an American man is currently about 65 years. This figure has increased by almost 300 percent in the last 200 years. Historically most people in America died from injury or disease, but today it is more likely that the cause of death will be old age. That is because most people in developed countries have relatively plentiful food, a high standard of living, and access to medical and dental care should they need it. As a result, people live longer. But they cannot avoid aging.

What causes aging?

For many years aging was simply thought of as a gradual process that occurred as humans passed the usual age of reproduction. Then in the 1960s scientists discovered that aging occurs at the cellular level. The results of their investigations seemed to indicate that many cells can only divide a fixed number of times. After about 50 divisions they can neither divide nor repair themselves. This state is called cellular senescence.

Most cells contain structures called chromosomes, which are made of deoxyribonucleic acid, or DNA. Lengths of DNA form genes, which drive the way a cell functions. Cellular aging is thought to be caused by a gradual shortening of the telomeres with each division. Telomeres are the end parts of the chromosomes on which there are no genes. Eventually telomeres get so short that cells cannot divide without losing genetic information.

Biologists have recently discovered a chemical called telomerase. Telomerase is an enzyme, a protein that powers chemical reactions in the body. It occurs in fetal germ cells. They are cells in a fetus that have yet to differentiate (become specialized cells). Telomerase can restore the telomeres so cells can still divide. The making of enzymes such as telomerase is controlled by genes on DNA. In time, it may be possible to switch the gene for telomerase production on or off. Scientists are researching the effects of such gene treatment.

LOOKING AFTER YOUR BODY

Aging is a natural process. As people get older, their appearance changes. But so too do their internal organs, which function less efficiently. People spend a lot of time and money making themselves look younger and hiding the physical signs of aging. Which do you think is more important—preserving your looks or taking care of organs such as your heart and lungs? Although looking after your internal organs is more important than how you look, there can be a positive mental benefit in looking after your appearance—if you feel good about yourself, you tend to be more active, which in itself is good for your heart and lungs.

Keeping active, both mentally and physically, is one of the best ways to battle the signs and symptoms of aging.

What does aging do?

As people grow older, their hair usually turns gray, and men sometimes go bald. Skin becomes drier, less elastic, and wrinkled, and it is less effective at regulating body temperature. This makes old people susceptible to conditions such as hypothermia (getting dangerously cold).

Muscle strength starts to decrease from about the age of 25, and by age 85 it has halved. People slowly lose height and might start to walk with a slight stoop. Bones weaken, and sometimes **osteoporosis** develops. It is a potentially serious condition in which bones become thinner, less dense, and more brittle. Osteoporosis is one of the major causes of hip fractures in people more than 65 years old. Preventative measures include doing regular exercise and making sure there is lots of calcium and vitamin D in the diet.

Senses deteriorate as people get older. Eyesight becomes less efficient, particularly if light levels are poor. Most old people need glasses for reading and distance vision. Hearing grows weaker from the age

of 30, but it is not usually until later in life that people realize they can no longer hear certain sounds. Eventually it may be necessary for a person to wear a hearing aid.

By the time people reach 60 years old, reactions are slower, concentration is more difficult, and some people might suffer from short-term memory loss. However, although brain tissue is lost as people grow older, many people are affected more by physical disabilities than mental ones.

SCIENCE WORDS

- **arthritis** Inflammation of the joints that causes pain, stiffness, and swelling.
- **osteoporosis** A medical condition in which the bones become weaker with age.
- **puberty** The process of developing from a child into an adult who can have children of his or her own.

GLOSSARY

allele Any of the alternative forms of a gene that may occur at a given point on a chromosome.

amino acid Nitrogen-containing molecule that is a building block of proteins.

arthritis Inflammation of the joints that causes pain, stiffness, and swelling.

asexual reproduction Any type of reproduction that produces offspring without involving mating or fertilization.

chromosome DNA-containing structure that forms by the joining of two identical chromatids during cell division.

clone An individual that has exactly the same genes as another individual. Asexual reproduction produces clones.

cytoplasm Contents of a cell outside the nucleus, excluding the cell membrane.

deoxyribonucleic acid (DNA) Molecule that contains the genetic code for all cellular (nonvirus) organisms.

diploid Cell or organism that contains two sets of chromosomes.

double helix Twisted ladderlike shape of a DNA molecule.

egg Haploid female sex cell.

embryo The early stage of an animal while it is in the egg or within the uterus of the mother. In humans the term refers to the unborn child until the end of the seventh week following conception.

enzyme Protein that speeds up chemical reactions inside an organism.

estrogen The most important female sex hormone. It controls the development of sexual characteristics.

F1 generation The young produced by a pair of test organisms. Their young are called the F2 generation.

fertilization The fusion of a sperm and an egg. It can occur externally (inside a body), as in mammals, or externally (outside the body), as in many fish.

fetus Unborn animal that is more developed than an embryo. In people the embryo becomes a fetus eight weeks after conception.

fission A type of asexual reproduction used by single-celled life-forms. In binary fission one cell divides into two. In multiple fission one cell divides into more than two daughter cells.

gene A segment of deoxyribonucleic acid (or DNA). Chromosomes, which are made of DNA, are passed from parents to young by sex cells.

generation The average span of time between the birth of parents and the birth of their offspring. About 25 years in people.

genome All the genes present inside an organism.

genotype The genes in an organism that code for a certain phenotype.

haploid A cell such as a sex cell (or, rarely, the cells of a whole organism, such as a male ant) that contains one set of chromosomes.

hermaphrodite An organism that has both male and female reproductive organs.

hormone Chemical messenger that is released inside the body to control life processes, such as development, growth, and reproduction.

inheritance The receiving of genes and their associated characteristics by young from their parents.

karyotype A visual profile of an organism's chromosomes, arranged in order of size.

life cycle The series of changes that life-forms undergo as they move from the youngest developmental stage to the creation of that same developmental stage in a subsequent generation.

life stage Distinct stages in an organism's life cycle. Larvae (young) such as caterpillars, tadpoles, fish fry, fly maggots, and beetle grubs are life stages. In mammals, birds, and reptiles the two main life stages (juvenile and adult) are less distinct.

mate When two individuals (the parents) come together to produce young.

meiosis Process of cell division that produces sex cells.

menstruation Period during which a female mammal discharges blood and sheds the thickened uterine lining. Only occurs in the absence of pregnancy.

messenger RNA (mRNA) Chemical that takes the genetic code from DNA in the nucleus to the ribosomes, where it becomes a template for protein production.

metamorphose To change physical form, especially when going from one life stage to another.

mitosis Process of cell division that leads to the production of body cells.

mutation A change in a cell's DNA.

nucleotide Part of a DNA molecule, comprising a sugar, a phosphate group, and a base.

nucleus Organelle that contains a cell's DNA.

organelle Membrane-lined structures, such as the nucleus, inside eukaryote cells.

osteoporosis A medical condition in which the bones become weaker with age.

ovary Female gonad, which produces egg cells.

ovulation The periodic release of unfertilized eggs in female animals, including people.

parthenogenesis A type of asexual reproduction in which a female produces young without a male's sperm to fertilize her eggs. Means "virgin birth."

phenotype A feature coded for by a gene.

placenta A blood-rich temporary organ in the uterus during pregnancy. It nourishes the embryo. Mammals and some fish, such as sharks, have placentas.

pollen Powder produced by male flowers that contains male sex cells.

polyploid Organism that contains more than two sets of chromosomes.

protein Molecule formed by amino acids in the ribosome.

puberty The process of developing from a child into an adult who can have children of his or her own.

replication Self-copying of a DNA molecule.

reproduction The way in which a life-form produces the next generation of young.

ribonucleic acid (RNA) Chemical similar to DNA involved in protein production.

ribosome Granule on which protein production occurs.

sex cell An egg or sperm. Sex cells (or gametes) have half as many chromosomes as body cells.

sexual reproduction Any type of reproduction that involves mating, fertilization, and the mixing of parental genes.

sperm Haploid male sex cell.

spermatophore A packet of sperm in a protective coating that a male animal leaves somewhere for a female to pick up.

spore An asexual reproductive cell that can develop into a new individual without being fertilized. Spores are produced by bacteria, fungi, and green plants.

testosterone The most important male sex hormone. It controls the development of sexual characteristics.

transcription The process of converting the coding sections of a DNA molecule into RNA.

transfer RNA (tRNA) Type of RNA that binds to amino acids and brings them to a ribosome for assembly into proteins.

uterus A stretchy muscular sac within which embryos develop during pregnancy.

zygote The fertilized egg created when an egg cell and a sperm fuse at conception.

FURTHER RESOURCES

PUBLICATIONS

Allan, T. *Understanding DNA: A Breakthrough in Science*. Chicago, IL: Heinemann Library, 2002.

Day, T. *Routes of Science: Genetics*. San Diego, CA: Blackbirch Press, 2004.

Harman, A. *Parasites and Partners: Farmers and Slavers*. Chicago, IL: Raintree, 2003.

Hoare, B. *Parasites and Partners: Breeders*. Chicago, IL: Raintree, 2003.

Morgan, S. *Body Doubles: Cloning Plants and Animals*. Chicago, IL: Heinemann Library, 2002.

Morgan, S. *Looking at Plants: Flowers, Fruits and Seeds*. London, UK: Belitha Press, 2002.

Parker, S. *In Your Genes: Genetics and Reproduction*. Chicago, IL: Heinemann-Raintree, 2007.

Sneddon, R. *Cells and Life: Cell Division and Genetics*. Chicago, IL: Heinemann library, 2002.

Spilsbury, R. *The Human Machine: Reproduction and Genetics*. Chicago, IL: Heinemann Educational Books, 2008.

Teacher Created Materials. *The World of Genetics*. Westminster, CA, 2008.

Yount, L. *Great Medical Discoveries: Gene Therapy*. San Diego, CA: Lucent Books, 2002.

WEB SITES

DNA From the Beginning
www.dnaftb.org/dnaftb
An animated primer on the basics of DNA, genes, and heredity, from the Dolan DNA Learning Center.

DNA Interactive
www.dnai.org/index.htm
See an interactive time line, learn how the code was cracked, and find out how the discovery of the structure of DNA changed the field of biology.

How Human Reproduction Works
www.howstuffworks.com/human-reproduction.htm
With text, diagrams, and links to other articles on related topics.

The Biology Project: Human Reproduction Problem Set
www.biology.arizona.edu/human_bio/problem_sets/Human_Reproduction/human_reproduction.html
Multiple-choice quiz on human reproduction with explanations. Incorrect answers are linked to tutorials to help solve the problem.

The Geee! in Genome
nature.ca/genome
More than 200 richly illustrated and interactive pages on genes, stem cells, genetically modified organisms, cloning, and the diversity of life. By the Canadian Museum of Nature.

The Life of Birds (Parenthood)
www.pbs.org/lifeofbirds/home/index.html
Learn about the diverse breeding strategies of birds.

INDEX